Hampshire & The Isle Of Wight

Edited by Mark Richardson

 Young**Writers**

First published in Great Britain in 2008 by:
Young Writers
Remus House
Coltsfoot Drive
Peterborough
PE2 9JX
Telephone: 01733 890066
Website: www.youngwriters.co.uk

SB ISBN 978-1 84431 737 0

Foreword

Young Writers' Big Green Poetry Machine is a showcase for our nation's most brilliant young poets to share their thoughts, hopes and fears for the planet they call home.

Young Writers was established in 1991 to nurture creativity in our children and young adults, to give them an interest in poetry and an outlet to express themselves. Seeing their work in print will encourage them to keep writing as they grow, and become our poets of tomorrow.

Selecting the poems has been challenging and immensely rewarding. The effort and imagination invested by these young writers makes their poems a pleasure to enjoy reading time and time again.

Contents

Holbrook Primary School

Kayleigh Long (8) 1
Hannah Smith (8) 1
Harriet Fox (11) 2
Courtney Read (9) 2
Sammy Ingledew (10) 3
Zoe Everett-Taylor (8) 3
Mollie Kinnoch & Abbie Kerrigan (10) 4
Lily Thorpe (9) 4
Kayley Taylor (11) 4
Ryan Ingledew (8) 5
Milly Roberts (9) 5
Annalise Daryl Maclellan (11) 5
Charlie Payne (9) 6
Kiera Keates (11) 6
Kaitlin Charlesworth (7) 7
Jessica Momen (10) 7
Lewis Alexander Haines (10) 7
Ailsa Speak (11) 8
Ethan Roberts (8) 8
Liam Mitchell (11) 8
Tilly Docherty (7) 9
Benjamin Godley (9) 9
Becky Ward (10) 10
Julian Frederick Mitchell (9) 10
George Heads & Oakley Richardson 11

Isambard Brunel Junior School

Jodie Chadwick (11) 11
Billie McClelland (11) 12
Aliya Gemechu (10) 12
Jade Chandler (11) 13
Katy McKee (11) 13
Katherine Kenward (11) 14
Bethany Ford (11) 14
Emily Brooks (11) 15
Kelly O'Rourke (11) 15
Meljude Fajardo (10) 16
Calvin Davies (10) 16

Simone Proudley (10)	17
Polina Vaino (10)	17
Courtney Barrasford (10)	18
James Bonsall (11)	18
Siân Rowe (11)	19
Ebony Binding (8)	19
Connor Sprake (10)	20
Zachary Drewry (8)	20
Summer Rivers (8)	21
Moriem Ahmed (10)	21
Jade Samways (10)	22
Casey Lister (9)	22
Rucksana Hoque (10)	23
Kara McGrath	23
Leanne Fowles (10)	24
Ronnie Chaplen (8)	24
Emily Cox (8)	25
Sophie Parsons (11)	25
Katie House (11)	26
Lucy Jones (7)	26
Chloe Planas (8)	26
Shayley Emmerson (11)	27
Jake Binding (10)	27
Sami Gemechu (7)	27
Lois Davies (7)	28

Longparish CE Primary School

Phoebe Dewbury (11)	28
Charlotte Hulme (10)	28
Esmé Parkins (11)	29
Jemma Dunford (11)	29
Jemima Shelley (11)	30
Tristan Flynn-Williams (11)	30
Robbie Pullan (9)	31
Harriet Stapleton (10)	31
Nathan James Fitter (9)	31
Yentl Love (10)	32
Aaron Wooltorton (9)	32
Rebecca Scarfe (10)	33

Marchwood Junior School

Emma Martin (11)	33
Megan Ford (11)	33
Maxine Andrassy (10)	34
Isabella White (10)	34
Grace Allinson (11)	35
Emma Louise White (11)	35
Christopher Toy (11)	36
Macey Towers (10)	36
Sam James (11)	37
Rebecca Emily Curtis (11)	37
Kathrine Sophocleous (9)	38
Amy Andrassy (11)	38
Jessica Bishop (9)	39
Jodie White (11)	39
Brittany Mae Welham (11)	40
Alix Trenerry (11)	40
Alexandra Dyke & Emily Middleditch (11)	41
Elizabeth Brewer (10) & Lillia Neale (11)	41
Phoebe Meredith & Emma Meadows (11)	42
Nicola Johnstone (10)	42
Cherise Biddleston (10)	43
Hannah Mabbett (10)	43
Jasmine-Jayde Corsham (10)	44
Alice Whitehorn (11)	44
Zoë Robinson (10)	45
Rosie Birkett-Wendes (9)	45
Stephanie Reed (11)	46
Katharyn Pennell & Caitlin Harris (11)	46
Emma Meadows (11)	47
Hannah Louise Ross (11)	47
Charlie Long (10)	48
Leanne Keily (11)	48
Kieren Farrell (9)	49
Callum Shearer & Gordon Golding (11)	49
Georgina Trueman (9)	50
Katharyn Pennell (11)	50
Elizabeth Amy Banks (10)	51
George Foster (10)	51
Georgia Hill (11)	51
Cullan Mitchell (9)	52

Charly-Jane Currie & Hettie Beale (11)	52
Ellie Bennett (8)	53
Perry Whitmarsh & Danielle Meffen (11)	53
Zoe Long (9)	54
Solomon Carr (10)	54
Rory Clements (10)	55
Abigail Dodds (10)	55
Kimberley Collins (10)	56
Maisie White & Emma Horsefield (8)	56
Matthew Edwards (10)	57
Charlotte Warner (10)	57
Katie Wood & Ria Twine (9)	58
Amy Fielding & Danielle Anderson-Webb (9)	58
Hannah Curtis (9)	59
Michael Guy (9)	59
Dan Colmer (9)	60
Christy Towers (9)	60
Thomas Austin (10)	61
Jamie Pidgley (9)	61
Leah Perkis (10)	62
Thomas Robinson (9)	62
Daniel Reed (10)	63
Leila Wallingford & Charlotte Landy (9)	63
Tristan Orchard (8)	64
Zoe Carroll	64
Charlotte White	64
Gracie Rose Walker (9)	65
Lisa Martin (9)	65
William Trueman (8)	65
Matthew Besant (9)	66
Dean Kuyser (9)	66
George Hibbs (9)	66
Lucy Tilt (9)	67
Ellie Penk (8)	67
Jack Whetren (10)	67
Neisha Rendell (9)	68
Abigail Deane (9)	68
Jack White (9)	69
Thomas Walsh (8)	69
Evan Meadows (9)	70
Jack Sardeña (10)	70

Sasha Owsnett (10)   71
Lucy Finch (10)   71

Medina Primary School
Daisy-May Palmer (9)   72
Elizabeth Davis (8)   72
Tilly Melda Westrope (8)   73
William Slade (8)   73
Rebecca Heath (8)   74
Holly Louise Legge (9)   74

Niton Primary School
Charlotte Phillips (9)   75
Ross Whyte (9)   75
Kimberley Trasler (9)   76

St Mary's CE Junior School, Basingstoke
William Taylor (9)   76
Charlie Lucas-Smith (9)   76
Merryn Heels (9)   77
Capryce Dunning (9)   77
Sam Western (8)   77
Harriet Fern (9)   78
Paul Surplice (9)   78
Rhianna Perkins (11)   79
Georgia King (9)   79
Alexander Drewry (11)   80
Abigail Fern (10)   80
Aidan Day (9)   81
Britney Boyd (8)   81
Michael Ash (9)   82
Jordan Lodomez (9)   82
Helen Frawley (11)   83
Jamie MacQuillin (8)   83
Tayla Porter (10)   84
Jasmine Symonds (8)   84
Amy Hermitage (9)   85
Katie Guo (8)   85
Jacob Bell (8)   85
Aaron Randall (9)   86
Harrison Crass (9)   86

Jordan Thorne (9)	87
Robert Sheldrake (9)	87
Holly Vary (9)	87
Lucy Bradley (9)	88
Luke Briggs (9)	88
Ashley Payne (11)	89
Matthew Comer (9)	89
Hannah Duncanson (10)	90
Lenny Rice (9)	90
Georgia Freeman (9)	91
Tom Turner (9)	91
Christy Chui (11)	92
Jack Randall (9)	92
Edward Quick (11)	93
Daisy Potter (8)	93
Maddie Merwin (11)	94
Tash Porter (9)	94
Charlie Taylor (11)	95
James Ash (11)	95
Georgia Beard (8)	96
Daniel Cochrane (8)	96
Charles Robertson (11)	96
Daniel Weir (11)	97
Jonathan Hyam (11)	97
Fraser McGregor (10)	97
Ryan Cochrane	98
Matthew Parry (9)	98
Hannah Best (10)	99
Reece Simper (10)	99
Naomi Hughes-White (11)	100
Alice Senior (11)	100
James Alford (11)	101
Jordan Ward (10)	101
Rhys John Poole (10)	102
Dominic Rodriguez (10)	102
Joseph Lane (10)	103
Amy Lillis (9)	103
Aldouz Parnada (10)	104
Bethany Layland (10)	104
Georgia Beeston (11)	105
Aditya Shrestha (11)	105
Dickson Chui (10)	106

Jemma Godleman (10)   106
Jody Patton (11)   106
James Smith-Cumming (11)   107
Charlie-Louise Batchelor (11)   107
Hannah Toogood (11)   107
Ashleigh Rheann Jones (11)   108
Andrew Gurr (11)   108
Sinead Grover (11)   109
Thomas Ash (11)   109

St Swithun's Primary School, Portsmouth
Lauren Nicholls (11)   110
Corey Almond (9)   110
Christopher Shore (9)   111
Katie Dalgleish (11)   112
Jistel Djeumo (11)   112
Joseph Hargreaves (10)   113
Annabel House (10)   113
Jacob Hillman-Illingworth (10)   114

St Swithun Wells Catholic Primary School
Niamh Colby (7)   114
Patrick Brewer (7)   114
Matthew Moules (10) & James Davis (11)   115
Melissa Dorrington (11)   116

The Poems

A Walk Round The Playground

I went for a walk in my playground
And guess what I saw . . .
Some disgusting litter
Dumped on the floor.

Some smelly Cheestrings packets
Some torn up tissue paper
A mini, mouldy milk carton.

A crumpled up crisp packet
Some sharp, broken glass
When we saw all this
We had to go back to class.

Kayleigh Long (8)
Holbrook Primary School

Save Our Planet

Recycle, recycle,
Listen to me,
Waste paper
Wastes trees,
Wastes trees,
Wastes trees,
Wastes bees.
Don't be silly,
Don't waste trees,
Don't put litter on the floor,
The planet will get ruined
If you drop more and more . . .

Hannah Smith (8)
Holbrook Primary School

War

War, what good can come of this?
Men are killed for the lives of me and you.
Guns shooting,
Ships sinking,
Bombs dropping
And all for what?
A country?
Food?
Or just plain life?
Sometimes we have no choice
But to fight, for freedom
And what is rightfully ours.
War,
It is neither life nor death.

Harriet Fox (11)
Holbrook Primary School

All About How To Save The Planet

Waste paper, wastes trees.
Do you want a rubbish world?
If you don't then start to recycle.

We can recycle cans, bottles, shoes and clothes.
Don't waste too much paper,
Because you are wasting too many trees.

Listen, listen, listen to me tell you how to recycle,
So that you are saving the planet.
The more we recycle the better the world will be.

Help us save the planet!

Courtney Read (9)
Holbrook Primary School

Save The Animals

S is for spider, with a silk web
A is for ants, looking after the eggs
V is for venomous snake, digesting its prey
E is for elephants, stamping on the earth.

T is for tiger, the silent hunter
H is for hippos, *never* disturb
E is for envy inside me.

A is for animals, great and small
N is for nocturnal owls, hooting at the moon
I is for iguana, laying in the sun
M is for mammals like me and you
A is for anger, growing inside me
L is for lion, so fierce
S is for the sun, burning out!

Sammy Ingledew (10)
Holbrook Primary School

Smelly Things That Belong In The Bin

I went for a lovely walk
On the field
And boy was I shocked.
All there was left was . . .
Mini, mouldy milk cartons,
Gooey, gloomy gum packets,
Curled, crushed Capri Sun drink,
A crumpled cardboard box!

All these horrible things
Belong in the bins!

Zoe Everett-Taylor (8)
Holbrook Primary School

Wildlife

W is for baby wallaby, in its mother's pouch
I is for insects, crawling on your couch
L is for leopard, looking for its prey
D is for dolphins, swimming all day
L is for llama, having fun
I is for iguanas, laying in the sun
Γ is for ferrets, chewing on your sleeve
E is for elephants, chewing on leaves.

Mollie Kinnoch & Abbie Kerrigan (10)
Holbrook Primary School

Recycle

R is for rubbish, pick yours up.
E is for environment, take care of your world.
C is for care, are you caring for your country?
Y is for yummy vegetables that people grow.
C is for considerate to the world?
L is for loving your garden.
E is for responsible for each other.

Lily Thorpe (9)
Holbrook Primary School

Recycle

R is for rubbish
E is for environment
C is for cars that don't want to be used
Y is for young people that walk to school
C is for clutter spreading over the world
L is for littering on the Earth
E is for the Earth being destroyed by people.

Kayley Taylor (11)
Holbrook Primary School

Rubbish Rap

The rubbish in the playground
Was so bad,
That when I looked at it again
I was so sad.
Didn't you listen to the recycling man,
That you have to put the rubbish in the van.
Please don't put the rubbish in the school
Because that is not very cool!

Ryan Ingledew (8)
Holbrook Primary School

Trees

I know we plant trees, it is very pretty
But why do you have to chop them down?
It makes it not a very nice city.

I know we make paper
But I don't know why we do
Because most people just waste it
All year through.

Milly Roberts (9)
Holbrook Primary School

Recycle

R is for rubbish
E is for the environment
C is for cars that don't need to be used
Y is for young people that walk to school
C is for clutter spreading all over the world
L is for littering on the Earth
E is for the Earth being destroyed by people.

Annalise Daryl Maclellan (11)
Holbrook Primary School

The Litter Nation

I was walking through the playground one day
When I found some disgusting things
It was all in the trees and bushes
Instead of the rubbish bins.

There were some crumpled up crisp packets
And a gooey chewing gum box
That was so revolting
They smelled like my mum's old socks.

There was also a mouldy milk carton
And a packet of cheese strings
The bad thing about it was
My friends like to eat these things.

There was also a squashed bottle of pop
And some small pieces of glass
Then we had the biggest problem of all
To pick it up was a task.

I really hate all this rubbish
It really makes my eyes sting
But if you see any rubbish
Please, put it in the bin!

Charlie Payne (9)
Holbrook Primary School

Recycling

R is for recycling
E is for everybody doing their best
C is for cycling and not driving
Y   is for you not wasting paper
C is for composting your snack rubbish
L is for not littering and having a good environment
E is for everybody, helping us with a
    Healthy planet!

Kiera Keates (11)
Holbrook Primary School

Be A Hero

Be a hero, make pollution zero
Be green
A hero is always green
And everyone will love you if you're a hero
Be green and make it be seen
By telling everyone about air pollution
Don't go by car when you can walk
And make sure your help is seen!

Kaitlin Charlesworth (7)
Holbrook Primary School

Recycle

R is for reuse
E is for the Earth being destroyed
C is for cars that should not be used
Y is for you to walk to school
C is for composting that we should all do
L is for legs that should be used
E is for food that should be eaten.

Jessica Momen (10)
Holbrook Primary School

Recycle

R is for rubbish that we should reuse
E is for the Earth that is getting destroyed
C is for cars that should not be used
Y is for young people who should walk to school
C is for cans that we can recycle
L is for legs that you should use to walk to school
E is for the Earth that is being abused.

Lewis Alexander Haines (10)
Holbrook Primary School

Koala Bear

K is for koalas in crisis.
O is for only surviving this minute.
A is for always gentle creatures.
L is for living in the wild
A is for all of us caring for them.

B is for bearing with us as we try to save you.
E is for everlasting freedom.
A is for fresh air floating all around them.
R is for rainforest and keeping their home.

Ailsa Speak (11)
Holbrook Primary School

Help The Environment

Help our environment, please.
If you waste paper you will waste trees.
If you waste a tree you will waste monkeys.
Then the monkeys will die.

Help the environment, please.
If you waste a shoe you will waste rubber.
If you waste rubber you will waste rubber trees,
Then your feet will hurt.

Ethan Roberts (8)
Holbrook Primary School

War

W is for war on the horrible field
A is for army, battling for their lives
R is for rest in peace.

War!

Liam Mitchell (11)
Holbrook Primary School

Six Things Someone Forgot To Put In The Bin

I went for a walk in the playground
And I was shocked,

I saw a . . .
    mini, mouldy milk bottle
    and a
    squashed cardboard box

Next I saw a . . .
    disgusting Coke bottle
    and a
    crumpled crisp packet

Then I saw a . . .
    gooey chewing gum box
    and a
    sharp, broken glass.

Sadly, we then went back to class.

Tilly Docherty (7)
Holbrook Primary School

The World

U nderstand racism, but never use it
N ever litter in our world
 I n our world there is racism
T reat others how you would like to be treated
E veryone should help keep our world clean
D ump your rubbish in a bin, not on the floor

K ill hatred not love
 I nsects matter more than us
N ever throw litter on the floor
G et recycling
D eep underground lay secrets
O xygen is important, help keep it clean
M ore we keep our environment clean the better we live.

Benjamin Godley (9)
Holbrook Primary School

Mr And Mrs Recycle

Mrs Corker is a very good walker
She doesn't like driving her car
She also likes to save energy, which makes her a star
But when she recycles her paper
She makes me feel a lot safer
That's why I like Mrs Corker.

Mr Man likes to fan all his golden hair
But he also likes to dump his old, rusty chairs
He should have recycled them, that would be better
He also doesn't know what to do with his letter.

Mrs Bin recycles tins
On her daily walks
When she spots a bit of litter
She never talks
She thinks rubbish is a disgrace
Everywhere, in every place.

Becky Ward (10)
Holbrook Primary School

Racism

R acism is wrong, do not do it
A nd stay away from groups that do it.
C ould say friendly things about other people
 I n all the ways you can.
S ome people are different and they can't help it.
M y group try to stop this happening.

Julian Frederick Mitchell (9)
Holbrook Primary School

Save Our Planet!

If you waste paper
You waste trees,
You might kill bees.
All your metal tins,
Don't put them in the bin.

George Heads & Oakley Richardson
Holbrook Primary School

Recycling Poem

Recycling is very important for our environment,
If you do well then well done to you, that's a step to saving the world.
We all know how to do it, but the thing is, do you want to do it?

Recycling, (which is very important), can be used over and over again.
We all know that paper comes from trees,
So the more paper we use we can recycle it,
Instead of using up all of the trees.
It is very important that we help our planet
Or otherwise we get global warming.

If you recycle at school and at home,
Well then, you are brilliant.
If we could get all the schools recycling
that would be a really great start.
We all have recycling bins at home,
So why not give it a try
And see if you can make a difference to the world.

Recycling - come on, why not give it a go?
See if you can make the world a better environment.

Jodie Chadwick (11)
Isambard Brunel Junior School

Green Journey

Green is the colour of the go light at the traffic signs,
Sat in my green car, waiting at the red, now green . . . *go!*
On my way I see children using the Green Cross Code.

Blurred green bushes rush past as I speed down the road,
Green bugs hit my windscreen as I get faster and faster,
We drive down a street lined with natural green hedges.

I drive and drive until I come to the Emerald Isle,
I'm running out of petrol . . . I stop and fill the tank
Using green, unleaded fuel.

I pass a Great Britain mini and my eyes turn green with envy,
The car is getting hot and the passenger is sick
With a face of pure green.

I do a big sneeze from my nose - green in colour,
I then realise it is on my clothes,
Then I get in my car and head to the green, green grass of home.

Billie McClelland (11)
Isambard Brunel Junior School

Poverty

Poverty means that the homeless can't pay,
So let's make the most of now you have something to say,
Think about when you put food to waste,
Other people have nothing to taste.

Appreciate that you are very lucky,
Others have water that is mucky!
Try all you can, be fair,
All you have to do is just share!

Make poverty history!

Aliya Gemechu (10)
Isambard Brunel Junior School

Homeless Poem

Homeless people must be sad
They must be lonely too.
They must be hungry
Because they have no money for food.

They must be sad because
They can't feed themselves and children too.
Sleeping in the dark, lonely through the night,
Lots of scary noise,
Getting wet in the winter,
Colder than can be.

Then sweating in the summer heat,
Not able to get clean.
Then when I see them
I think of me, if I were them
When I see them
I feel sad inside
And then I want to help them.

Jade Chandler (11)
Isambard Brunel Junior School

Recycling

People go to the recycling bank,
It smells like fish gone rank.

Mums help by going to the compost bin,
All the mouldy fruit gets chucked in.

Compost makes lots of soil
And earthworms end up in a coil.

I will help the planet go green,
If I turn off the TV screen!

Katy McKee (11)
Isambard Brunel Junior School

Can We Fix It?

There's a sea of litter on the floor,
Cars pollute our cities like a fire-breathing dragon,
Wildlife disappears as trees are cut down,
Can we fix it?

We *will* use the bins in our streets,
We *will* walk or cycle to our destination,
We *will* reuse, recycle and reduce rubbish,
We *will fix it!*

The streets sing our praises as
We help them breathe again,
Our city's air is clear,
Our wildlife reappears, happy and jolly,
Our trees have a chance to grow,
We have fixed it!

Katherine Kenward (11)
Isambard Brunel Junior School

Help The World

Recycling is so much fun,
One click, consider it done.
Recycling all around you,
I will even recycle too.

Litter, litter all around,
Across the city it is found.
So pick it up off the floor
And don't be so poor.

Bang, bang, all around,
People screaming from under ground.
So help the world, the happier it will be,
For you and me!

So ask yourself - will you help the world?

Bethany Ford (11)
Isambard Brunel Junior School

Making The World A Better Place

You have to treat the world with care,
Or you will have the choice of it not being there.
No one wants to see the sun crash and burn,
But if you stop now it will all turn.

Everyone says we're doing just fine,
But really that is a lie,
Everyone tries to do their best,
Some people think that there's no one to do the rest.

Let's help the environment,
By doing our bit.
However it's only for our own benefit.

We all need to work together
To keep our planet green.
For one day,
It may not be seen.

Emily Brooks (11)
Isambard Brunel Junior School

Think Green

T o make the world a better place you must:
H elp pick up litter from the floor
 I t may seem like a massive bore
N evertheless it helps make a difference
K eeping the animals safe; that makes sense!

G reen bins mean only one word
R ecycling, should always heard
E ven recycling a bit each week
E xcelllent recycling will make you unique
N ow is the time to save the world

Remember, it's the place where we dwell!

Kelly O'Rourke (11)
Isambard Brunel Junior School

Litter Poem

Litter on the pavements,
Litter in the park,
Litter on the roads
And then it gets trampled by the cars.

Pollution will overcome our land
And that's not what we want,
So help us pick up every single piece of litter,
So we will once again triumph.

Litter will carry on forever,
Until the end of the world,
So why not recycle?
It's much, much easier,
Then the recycling men will collect it from your door.

What I'm trying to say is
That you should recycle
Instead of dropping litter on the floor.

Meljude Fajardo (10)
Isambard Brunel Junior School

War

Guns firing loud
As the army soldiers bowed
The birds flew by
As the guns shot high in the sky.

Men screaming loud
As the bullets crossed their brow
The man got shot and fell down
In the dark and lonely town.

The war is over
At the white cliffs of Dover.

Calvin Davies (10)
Isambard Brunel Junior School

Disease

Disease, it's all around.
It goes up, down and everywhere.
The people don't want to be ill,
But the disease hits you unexpectedly.
Diseases, diseases, they are all around,
When you go up and when you go down.
The plague, smallpox, haemorrhoids too,
These are all diseases and they come after you.

You breathe in the germs, they make you ill,
All over the world it happens.
You get very ill, it makes you cry,
You beg God that you don't die.
You suffer unhappy, some recover,
But some others don't.

You live your life unhappy and sad,
You breathe in some germs, it makes you ill,
You get sick and can't go on,
You suffer, unhappy,
It's the end for you.

Simone Proudley (10)
Isambard Brunel Junior School

Care

We should care about the others,
We should always do,
If we try all our hardest
We shall make it through.

So we'll have a rest,
Then we'll try our best,
So everyone
Will enjoy themselves.

Polina Vaino (10)
Isambard Brunel Junior School

Being Homeless

How would you feel if you had no home
And you slept in a cardboard box
And didn't own a mobile phone,
That's how life is for me.

No family or friends,
No hot baths for me
And no big screen TV,
That's how life is for me.

No school, yippee!
No internet, no books,
No cake for tea,
That's how life is for me.

No changing clothes,
No school discos,
No birthday teas,
No Christmas trees,
That's how life is for me.

Courtney Barrasford (10)
Isambard Brunel Junior School

Save The World

Here we are now,
With Earth's cries all around,
With the seas rising up,
There's no time to mess up!

Recycle our paper to save the trees,
Stop the world being brought to its knees!
Turn down the heat to stop the ice caps from melting,
Fight pollution to stop the acid rain pelting!

Now you see what you can do,
Join in now and make it true!

James Bonsall (11)
Isambard Brunel Junior School

Our World Is Dying

Animals in fear of extinction,
Poaching is the cause,
Rare species are dying out,
We are losing animals,
Our world is dying.

Trees are being cut,
Rainforests destroyed,
Many animals homeless,
Cutting back things we need,
Our world is dying.

Animals are wonderful creatures,
Lovely in every way,
Being killed for skins or meat,
Sold like dolls in a store,
Our world is dying.

Help stop these things,
Help start over and keep rare animals,
Stop our world from dying.

Siân Rowe (11)
Isambard Brunel Junior School

Homeless

The poor man sits alone,
On the corner of the street,
His only possession a cardboard box,
He holds out his hands,
Hoping that someone will give him some money,
But no one sees him there,
Maybe tomorrow will be a better day.

Ebony Binding (8)
Isambard Brunel Junior School

The Tramp

There was a man
With clothes all old
Holes in his shoes
Sat, freezing cold

Teeth all mangy
Hair all frizzy
Fingers all dirty
The smell makes you dizzy

From a dirty bottle
He's drinking beer
But does not care
As it brings him cheer

Tonight, when it's dark
He will sleep rough
But being homeless
Makes him tough . . .

Or does it?

Connor Sprake (10)
Isambard Brunel Junior School

Litter

L ittering is bad, it makes me mad.
I wish they used the bins and stopped dropping their tins.
T ell your friends to stop, you might get caught by a cop.
T ake your litter to the bin, soon it will be up to your chin.
E veryone is a winner, and the streets would be cleaner.
R emember your streets would be cleaner if you didn't litter.

Zachary Drewry (8)
Isambard Brunel Junior School

Being Homeless

I'm unhappy as I have been
thrown out of my house.
I am sad and lonely.
I am not rich as I have spent
all of my money.
I am so hungry
I could eat for days.
I have no bed and I sleep
In a cardboard box.
The weather is too hot and
I have got sunburnt,
but I have nowhere to go.
There is no water,
so I have a dirty face.
People stare at me as they walk past.
I need a home.

Summer Rivers (8)
Isambard Brunel Junior School

Litter

Litter is everywhere
Inside, outside
It's always there
To help the environment
Pick up some litter.

Everyone, come do it with me
Remembering litter if from you and from me.

Moriem Ahmed (10)
Isambard Brunel Junior School

Animals And Extinction

Animals and extinction
Bless their souls and hearts.
We have to save them
You can incredibly help
These poor little animals
From go-karts!

Birds, horses, mice and dogs
Feed them, please!
This has to stop
Full stop.

Whipped, lashed, starved
Ouch! Ouch! Ouch!
No sleep, no rest
Worldwide cruelties.

Jade Samways (10)
Isambard Brunel Junior School

Pollution

Pollution isn't an illusion
We did it, it's collusion.
Let us stop the chain reaction
We need to have a plan of action.

Global warming, is it here to stay?
If we work together it might go away.
Let's take action, let's get smart,
Don't let the Earth just fall apart.

Walk to school or ride a bike,
Tell your dad to take a hike.
When next at home just steal his keys
And hide them in the bottom of the deep freeze.

Casey Lister (9)
Isambard Brunel Junior School

The World

Make your world cool,
By not being a fool.
Racism is bad,
It will make you really sad.

By recycling you'll be great,
The world will be your mate.
You should be a pal,
Not be destroying!
Try stopping it now!

I hope you care,
Your thoughts should be shared.
Spread the word about the world,
So everyone can work together.

Rucksana Hoque (10)
Isambard Brunel Junior School

Make It Better

Why, oh why do you have to litter?
It makes the people very bitter.
Every bit of litter makes a heart go,
What animal? We will never know.

Don't use your car if it's not that far,
Walking is better and keeps you fitter.

Put your rubbish in a bin,
Then it won't be so glum.
Remember your bin is always there,
So don't put litter everywhere.

Poverty needs to be stopped,
So they can be happy and be with their family.
Poverty isn't funny,
Because they need help with money.

Kara McGrath
Isambard Brunel Junior School

Recycle Poem

M an-made
A chievable
K indness
E xtinction

T rees
H ealth
E veryone

W orldwide
O ngoing
R ules
L earning
D estruction

A nimals

B acklash
E ducation
T raining
T alking
E co-system
R esurrection

P lanet
L ove
A ffects
C ommunication
E nvironment.

Leanne Fowles (10)
Isambard Brunel Junior School

Poverty

People crying, people dying,
Helping each other to survive,
So they can stay alive.
I wish I could help them,
I wish I could give them some toys.

Ronnie Chaplen (8)
Isambard Brunel Junior School

Endangered Me

Help me. help me, help me please,
I'm a big elephant eating the leaves.
Here comes a band of men with loaded guns,
Killing me and my friends for our very big tusks.

Help me, help me, help me I beg,
I'm a polar bear with a very sore leg.
The ice is melting all around me,
My cubs need food, but there's too much sea.

Help me, help me, help me please,
I'm a leatherback turtle living in the sea.
Here come the humans with big, scary nets,
Scooping my friends up, I could be next.

They're also on the beach, taking my eggs,
I am frightened because there's so few of us left.
The sun is getting closer, drying up the sea,
The litter that is on the beach is choking me!

Emily Cox (8)
Isambard Brunel Junior School

Save The World

Stop pollution
And plant more trees
Vanish pollution by riding your bike
Everybody should be green

The world could be a better place
Homeless and worthless, never the best
Everybody should have a place in life

World, world could be cleaner
Other people should try harder
Recycle, recycle, more the better
Life is rough when no colour is around
Dull and miserable when everyone's down.

Sophie Parsons (11)
Isambard Brunel Junior School

Pick It Up

Pick it up, you know what I mean
If you don't, your roads won't be clean
When your dog goes for a poo
Please, pick it up, you don't live in a zoo!

It makes me feel mad
It makes me feel sad
Pick it up off the floor
Or you will have the police at your door.

Katie House (11)
Isambard Brunel Junior School

Litter

Litter, litter, all over the place,
Let's pick it up before it gets dark.
In the bin the litter must go,
As the grass will even grow.
Little babies play in the park,
Don't want them picking up something sharp.
Keep our park nice and clean,
We don't want litter, we want it to gleam.
We all love the clean park,
Quick, let's get home before it gets dark.

Lucy Jones (7)
Isambard Brunel Junior School

Litter

L ots of rubbish everywhere.
I t is causing pollution.
T oo many people noticing it but just leaving it.
T o make our world look better.
E verybody should pick it up.
R emember, if you see it, pick it up and put it in a bin.

Chloe Planas (8)
Isambard Brunel Junior School

Making The World A Better Place

To make the world a better place
Banish war without a trace.

Global warming is a warning
So turn your lights off in the morning.

Recycle as much as you can
A cleaner land is up to man.

To make the world a better place
Enjoy the world with all its space.

To carry on the human race
Let's make the world a better place!

Shayley Emmerson (11)
Isambard Brunel Junior School

Litter Everywhere

There's litter on the pavements.
There's litter in the road,
Empty cans moving on their own,
Carrier bags stuck up in the tree,
Making a noise as if to say,
When will someone come and rescue me?

Jake Binding (10)
Isambard Brunel Junior School

Litter

L ittering hurts animals.
I do not like to see littering.
T ry to recycle your litter.
T ry to save energy.
E veryone could pick up their litter.
R ecycling is good for the environment.

Sami Gemechu (7)
Isambard Brunel Junior School

Litter

L itter makes the streets look a mess.
I think we should get Gordon Brown to address.
T atty, noisy litter, rustling in the kerb.
T ime to tidy up and brush away the mess.
E nvironment we are polluting.
R ecycle our rubbish to save our world.

　　Replant, regrow, recycle!

Lois Davies (7)
Isambard Brunel Junior School

Hunting Orang-utans

The spring flowers open with bloom,
The bumblebees pass with a buzzing tune.
As I sit in my tree, keeping away,
All I have had today is the hunters,
Trying to chase me away.
People cut down our homes,
So they can use it for things.
So help us get away,
It will really make my day.

Phoebe Dewbury (11)
Longparish CE Primary School

Little Animals

A nimals deep in the jungle
N eed shelter from the sky
I nside a big jungle, shy
M any animals live outside
A ll different animals live in the jungle
L ive in such different ways
S uch as a little duck flapping its way in the sky.

Charlotte Hulme (10)
Longparish CE Primary School

Wouldn't It Be Nice . . .

Wouldn't it be nice to get away from the sound
Cars being used
Jammed in queues
Engines always on
Just droning along
Chug, chug, chug, like a motorboat
On rough ground 4 x 4s just float
Wouldn't it be nice to get away from the sound
And get all of the cars to the pound?
The world would be a much nicer place
Taking in the sights at our own pace
There wouldn't be such a dark cloud over our lives
'I've got to get the car fixed.'
What a surprise!
Saving money and oil
Helping the planet not come to the boil.

Esmé Parkins (11)
Longparish CE Primary School

Recycle And Don't Litter

R ecycle what you don't need.
E very bit of litter on the ground makes the world a bigger landfill.
C ans, paper, cartons, the lot can be recycled.
Y ou need to be careful, the world may go like a shooting star.
C ome, the environment needs your help by recycling.
L ots go into landfill, but not everything needs to be there.
E veryone will be sad to see the world go, so recycle
   and you will see the difference.

L ots of litter on the ground,
I n the bin there is no rubbish.
T he animals get stuck from the litter you drop
T ime goes by, there will be litter everywhere.
E verybody should throw away, but they leave it on the ground.
R ound the corner is a bin, they're too lazy to walk that far.

Jemma Dunford (11)
Longparish CE Primary School

The River

The river, happy, dancing and rippling,
Like a tap dancer quickly leaping.
In and out of the curling currents,
Reaching the Amazon forest.

Once he got there what a fright!
This simply was not right,
Half of the rainforest was bare,
They simply didn't care.

The river sad,
Feeling not so good,
Not at all in the mood.
Let's go somewhere,
Somewhere where they are trying,
Trying to help.
Yelp!

Jemima Shelley (11)
Longparish CE Primary School

I Wish . . .

The generals would stop the pop, pop at the nation of Iraq.
Then all the men could have a great lark in their newly built park.

I wish . . .
The men in the rainforest would stop chop, chop
And the wood would chop, chop, stop.
Then the chop, chop would stop, stop
And they'll have a lollipop.

I wish . . .
The cops would stop the lollipops from being thrown on the ground,
So lollipops in the Amazon would never be found.

I wish it would stop!

Tristan Flynn-Williams (11)
Longparish CE Primary School

Help Us

We need your help.
People's lives are hanging like a bead.
By donating money for the poor,
So they can get much more.
You must do your bit,
To save the people who have been hit.
If we do our bit we can help millions
Who think water, food and shelter are a dream.
If we can help the people who help the poor,
We can do much more!

Robbie Pullan (9)
Longparish CE Primary School

Water

The water shimmered like fish scales in the deep blue sea.
The dolphins splished and splashed.
The boats were bobbing up and down under the moonlit sky.
The nets dropped down and the dolphins got caught.
Now they're dying, so please help!

Harriet Stapleton (10)
Longparish CE Primary School

Clouds From The Water

C louds soar but do not die, flying over the bright blue sky.
L ofty, softy, fluffy clouds.
O bey the wind, unlike a bird, soaring fast but not heard.
U ndertaking the thirsty bird.
D own over the town, always smiling, never frowns.
S tupid, stupid pollution you are such a nuisance.

Nathan James Fitter (9)
Longparish CE Primary School

The Special Tree

Green, lush rainforest,
home to many animals of every colour and size.
Things that fly, crawl, walk or slither,
all living in one tree.

Then, as noisily as a baby cuckoo,
a monster came into the clearing,
would our special tree be cut down?
No, but others would.

The special tree survived this time,
but would it survive another raid?

As dawn broke, the monster came again,
as hungry as ever and began to kill things.

Crash, bang! down went our special tree,
like so many others, leaving the creatures homeless.

So stop, that's all we're asking,
Stop!

Yentl Love (10)
Longparish CE Primary School

Trees

T rees, cut down every day, roughly about ten a day, all of the trees
are pulled down by a rope and bulldozer
R oads are bare, no homes for woodpeckers, gulls, pigeons,
blackbirds and their babies, no food for woodpeckers.
E els can get their moisture from the swamps, no moisture; no eels.
E ggs have no place to be laid; no more animals!

Aaron Wooltorton (9)
Longparish CE Primary School

Now The Trees Are Gone

T errible trouble in the world
   Trees going down one by one.
R oads are bare, nothing to see,
   Can travelling be so boring to watch?
E ating our lives away, nothing around,
   Trees are not colourful, not now they've died.
E ggs have no nests,
   Starting to hatch.
S wallows come swooping down like a stone in a pond,
   Sounding like a crack, there's a new baby swallow in the sky.

Rebecca Scarfe (10)
Longparish CE Primary School

The Happy And The Sad Bin

The sad little bin, bin who had no litter,
The happy bin was so hungry he ate all the litter.

The sad bin was in pain, his tummy hurt really badly,
The happy bin was so greedy he ate all he could.

The sad bin was in tears,
Because he was very hungry.

Emma Martin (11)
Marchwood Junior School

The Dangerous Potion

An undiscovered object staring at the sea
It didn't realise that it was about to kill me.
The dangerous potion began to swim,
Then it came closer, near my brother Tim.
Later on I found my mum dying,
I didn't know what to do, so I started crying.

Megan Ford (11)
Marchwood Junior School

Save The Animals

Save the animals,
So scared,
So afraid,
So lonely.

Save the animals,
Keep them safe,
Keep them happy,
Keep them wild.

Save the animals,
Leave them alone,
Leave them to run free,
Leave them with us.

Save the animals,
It's their home,
It's our world,
It's your choice.

Save the animals.

Maxine Andrassy (10)
Marchwood Junior School

Save Our World

Save our world, by keeping nature happy.
Of course don't forget to keep Mother Nature happy.

Recycling is much better than throwing paper in a bin.
Or you could save trees by recycling things.

Saving power is also great,
Like turning off lights and saving heat.

In icy lands lots of ice is melting,
Penguins, bears, seals are dying.

We can stop all this happening
And keep the wide world happy.

Isabella White (10)
Marchwood Junior School

The Mega Machine

People dying of disease,
No one having home keys.
Blankets of litter everywhere,
Nothing is bare.

The world is warming,
'Cause everyone's touring.
Melting the ice round the polar bears' lair,
No one seems to care.

Planting crops,
While workers chop
Down the forest,
Till it's gone.

Save the world,
You know you can,
Recycle everything,
Including you!

Grace Allinson (11)
Marchwood Junior School

One Day

One day, when I am old enough,
I will work for NASA.
I will be a scientist
And build a rocket to send to Mars.
We will transport the population of this Earth,
When the Earth is dead and gone

One day we will destroy the planet Mars
And we will transport the population of Mars
To Saturn and carry on like this,
Until one day there is nothing left.
One day we will be the cause of our own deaths.

Emma Louise White (11)
Marchwood Junior School

Help

Our grass stays green
So don't be mean
Keep the rainforest
Nice and clean.

CO_2 is on the move
That means we need to improve
If we do that it's good for us
Then we won't breathe in the dust.

Litter, litter everywhere
Then people will stop and stare
If we clean up all the mess
Then our world will be the best.

Thank you everyone
Now is the time to end
The racism
And everything else.

Christopher Toy (11)
Marchwood Junior School

Racism

So you take helpless people for granted?
They can't help being different.
They're just the same as you!
So what about the outside,
It's the inside that counts!
Everybody has feelings,
Just like you and me.
So do unto others as you would want them to do to you.
Stop this racism!

Macey Towers (10)
Marchwood Junior School

Recycling And Pollution

Recycle the paper and card
But check the cans,
Don't put things in the wrong bin,
Recycle because it helps.

Use recycled paper,
Do as much as possible on one sheet of paper.
Try to buy recycled items,
Recycle because it helps.

Cycle to work or school, or maybe walk.
Use the shortest route to your destination.
Get as many people into as few cars as possible,
Turn the engine off at lights.

Only top up on petrol when there's barely any left in the tank.
Turn off the TV at the wall,
Turn off lights when you're not in the room.

Sam James (11)
Marchwood Junior School

Nature Tree

Look at the tree
What can you see?
The golden leaves swaying in the wind,
With a strong, brown trunk.

Look at the tree
What can you hear?
The leaves crunching together as I walk,
Birds, singing on the branches.

All these things are so beautiful,
So don't cut down trees,
So there will be life for everyone.

Rebecca Emily Curtis (11)
Marchwood Junior School

It's A Shame

It's a shame to see our world burn.
It's a shame to see our world die.
So please help, help us please.

It's a shame that people have no home.
It's a shame they have no family.
So please help, help us please.

It's a shame people cut down trees for crops,
It's a shame some countries are poor.
So please help, help us please.

It's a shame to see our animals die.
Help them be cured, make them well.

So you've heard what I've had to say,
So you do something,
Together we can make the world better.

Kathrine Sophocleous (9)
Marchwood Junior School

Not Long

Not long
Until the birds stop singing their song.

Not long
Until soil turns to oil.

Not long
Until my daughter drowns in deadly water.

Not long
Until gas pollutes the air, because you don't care.

Not long
For you to save the world.

Amy Andrassy (11)
Marchwood Junior School

Homeless And Helpless

Think about no water,
Think about no food,
Everyone just dying,
As the day passes through.

Think about no home,
Think about no friends,
Everyone just dying,
As the day passes through.

Everyone around,
Not a care in their mind,
But you make it better
And think, you've been kind.

Jessica Bishop (9)
Marchwood Junior School

The Happy Bin Who Had Eaten All The Litter

I love my litter, it is yummy,
I never want to leave my mummy.
Oh please, be quick, I am hungry,
All of it is scrummy, yum yum.

Throw your rubbish into my mouth,
I will crunch it up for you,
So every morning I will be ready,
I will eat it all up for you.

Remember, remember,
Recycle, recycle,
My little green brother loves paper,
Card and plastics.

Jodie White (11)
Marchwood Junior School

Reuse, Recycle

Reuse, recycle,
That's what I say
Egg boxes
Milk cartons
Do it all the way.
Help us make a better world
To show us the rights
Not the wrongs

We would be helping the world
Be a better place
Reuse anything
Recycle everything

Help stop pollution
War and extinction
Make the world understand

Show us the right thing to do!

Brittany Mae Welham (11)
Marchwood Junior School

The More

The more we save the planet
the planet, the planet.
The more we save the planet,
the happier we will be.
Pollution and gases
are ruining the Earth.

Alix Trenerry (11)
Marchwood Junior School

Animal Fury

Think!
How many animals are becoming extinct because of us?

Making lipstick,
Making polish,
Harms the un-harmful giant of the sea.
Hunting whales,
Just for fun,
Washes . . .
The whales' life away,
The sea is lonely without the whales' fun.

Seals flop around helplessly,
Trying to find food,
But there is no food around,
Seals are disappearing one by one.

Think!

Alexandra Dyke & Emily Middleditch (11)
Marchwood Junior School

Why, Why, Why

'Why, why, why?'
you hear them cry
and you still carry on
like it's a bunch of fun.

Chinchillas crying,
cheetahs dying,
can't you see,
they're going down in history.

Elizabeth Brewer (10) & Lillia Neale (11)
Marchwood Junior School

A Close Call

White ice,
Glistening in the sun,
All is still,
Polar bears wander,
Wondering why their home
Is being destroyed.

Snap!
A piece of ice breaks away,
The polar bear cub cries out,
His mother comes swimming,
Desperate to get him back.
Reaching the ice,
Mother grabs him,
He is safe.
This is happening as you read,
Because of *global warming,*
Let's save the polar bears
While we can!

Phoebe Meredith & Emma Meadows (11)
Marchwood Junior School

Put Your Litter In The Bin

Put your litter in the bin,
If you don't the world will die.
Put your litter in the bin,
If you don't the world will not win.

Put your litter in the bin,
If you don't the war we will not win.
Put your litter in the bin
If you don't the litter will win.

Nicola Johnstone (10)
Marchwood Junior School

Homeless

Please, please, save people from dying
And give them food,
It's not fair they're out there.
Let them be free
And give them a little hand.
They have to be free,
Please, please, they need help,
They need us.
Now people hurt them,
It's destroying their life.
They will not live any longer.
People, people,
They sometimes sleep on benches or on the floor.
They pick food from the bin,
Which is all food that has gone off.

Cherise Biddleston (10)
Marchwood Junior School

Pollution

Put your litter in the bin,
Observe the world that is surrounding us.
Leave your carbon footprint as it is,
Let the world be free.

Unlock the door to a perfect world,
Tell the world,
Icebergs melting,
Obey the world's rules,
Never destroy the world.

If everyone helps
We can make a big difference!

Hannah Mabbett (10)
Marchwood Junior School

Save The World

People are homeless, with nothing to eat,
People are in wars, ready for defeat.
Save the world.

Give money to charity,
To those who can't afford their tea.
Save the world.

Save the rainforests that are alight,
Which gives the animals a terrible fright.
There is one key to set these people free,
From all the terrible disease.

Think of you and me, we are lucky.
Save the world!

Jasmine-Jayde Corsham (10)
Marchwood Junior School

What Would We Do?

What would we do without any water?
What would we do without any food?
What would we do without any rainforest?
What would we do without any animals?
What would we do without any recycling?
If we didn't have anything in the world, the world would be a disaster.

If we had no water we would die of thirst.
If we had no food we would die of hunger.
If we had no rainforest several animals wouldn't have homes.
If we had no animals there would no nice, warm clothes.
If we had no recycling bins the world would be a dump.

If there was nothing in the world the world would disappear.

Alice Whitehorn (11)
Marchwood Junior School

Recycling

Recycling, recycling,
Recycle, recycle everything
Bottles, books, shoes and clothes,
Games and toys, plastic, card and board.
Anything you don't want, give, give, give,
Give to other children
Other children will love what you give.
Paper and cardboard use again,
Don't put it in the black bin,
Put it in the see-through bin.
Tins and jars put it in the bin,
Not in the black bin,
Whatever you do,
Recycle, recycle, recycle.

Zoë Robinson (10)
Marchwood Junior School

Animals In Danger

Today nature is dying!
Animals are getting killed!
So stop that hunting, please, please.

How do you think the animals feel?
You would not like it if I came along
Shot you and made you bleed.

Today nature is dying!
Animals are getting killed!
Let nature take its place,
Let animals die naturally,
We've done our bit, now you do yours.
It's your choice.
Save our World!

Rosie Birkett-Wendes (9)
Marchwood Junior School

Earth Will Not Be Here Forever

Litter lying, loitering,
No one to pick it up.

Plastic bottles, loads of glass
Thrown in the bin.

Pollution killing
Caused by transport fumes.

Animals endangered,
Made so by climate change.

Countries declaring war,
Poverty-stricken towns.

It all needs to be changed,
Otherwise the world will be no more.

Recycle, recycle,
Plastic, card, glass and much more.
The world would be turned around.

All that will be left
Is a cloud of rubbish,
Nothing left alive.

If we do not stop this
We will kill the world.

Stephanie Reed (11)
Marchwood Junior School

Tick-Tock

Day by day
Hour by hour
Minute by minute
Bang!
There goes the world
Help me!
I'm dying!

Katharyn Pennell & Caitlin Harris (11)
Marchwood Junior School

A Close Call

White ice,
Glistening in the sun,
All is still.
Polar bears wander,
Wondering why their home
Is being destroyed.
Snap!
A piece of ice breaks away,
The polar bear cub cries out.
His mother comes swimming,
Desperate to get him back.

Reaching the ice,
Mother grabs him,
He is safe!
This is happening,
As you read,
Because of *global warming*.
Let's save the polar bears while we can.

Emma Meadows (11)
Marchwood Junior School

How Would You Feel

How would you feel
If you were forced to live on
The dusty, old street
Without your loving family?

How would you feel
If you hadn't had food for weeks
And you were dying of thirst
And some of your family were becoming sick?

How would you feel if you were in an earthquake,
You were trapped in your house
And nobody was bothered to save you?

Hannah Louise Ross (11)
Marchwood Junior School

Animals In Danger

All the animals sleep and hide
But all the polar bears cry and cry.

If you love animals
Free them, save them, make them live.

All the pollution comes from cars,
How would you like it
If a cloud melted your island?

If you love animals,
Love them, save them, make them live,
Pollution is riding in the air,
You could kill a polar bear.

If you love animals,
Love them, save them, make them live.

Charlie Long (10)
Marchwood Junior School

Litter

Have you ever dropped litter?
Litter such as,
Cans?
Packets?
Fish hooks?
Ring pulls?
If you keep doing this the world will die
Under a cloud of rubbish.
So make sure you recycle all your rubbish.
There will be nowhere to put it,
Landfill sites will be full.
If we don't stop we will kill the world.

Leanne Keily (11)
Marchwood Junior School

War

If we stopped war, if we stopped war
There'd be no more of this.
Fighting is wrong, fighting is wrong.
I want to do something about it.
Don't die, don't die tonight,
Please stop war, please stop war,
Cos if we did we'd all be happy.

War, oh war, is banging at your door.
Questioning you to come for more.
If we stopped, if we stopped,
That would be the end of it.

Why, oh why, why, oh why?
This is a disgrace,
Why are we fighting?
Why are we fighting?
I do not know.

Kieren Farrell (9)
Marchwood Junior School

Reg, The Recycle Man

Reg, the recycle man
He sees everything
The paper in the black bin
He swaps to the green bin.

Glass, shimmering in golden sun
Veg, put it in the compost Reg
Paper, recycle it in a green bin
Card and plastic too.

Remember Reg,
Recycle
Possibilities are endless.

Callum Shearer & Gordon Golding (11)
Marchwood Junior School

So, Go Green

How would you feel having water at your door?
With sewage in the water
Water dirty enough to spread diseases
    So, go green!

With endangered animals being killed
Litter destroying their homes
Animals being hurt by litter
    So, go green!

How would you feel with a war near your home?
No food, no water
Waking up to the sound of guns.
    So, go green!

Pollution in the air
Trees destroyed by forest fires
Trees cut down for paper, cardboard and plastic
Icebergs melting
Reduce, reuse, recycle
It's better for our world!

Georgina Trueman (9)
Marchwood Junior School

Dear God

Dear God,
the one thing you ask
we have not done.
The clean air is running out,
the ice is gone,
we have tried
but not succeeded.
Tick-tock,
it's all gone.

Katharyn Pennell (11)
Marchwood Junior School

Sad Life

People living on the unfriendly streets,
Begging money, in a cardboard box,
Alleys crowded with homeless people,
Feeling like a piece of dirt.

Cardboard boxes wedged in shop doorways,
Only carrying the house in a carrier bag,
Wandering around, street to street,
Not any food to eat.

Elizabeth Amy Banks (10)
Marchwood Junior School

Global Warming

Polar bears, searching in vain for land.
The humungous icebergs collapsing and melting.
The furious ocean, rising, whilst getting warmer.
Cars producing smoke, which rises into the air.
Penguins, waddling to safe land.
Seals hoping that mankind will solve their mistake
Of global warming.

George Foster (10)
Marchwood Junior School

The Pollution Beast

Pollution is like an angry beast,
Blowing its gruesome breath over the land.
It's like he's picking up the Earth with his hand.
Please help me shoo him away!
By passing my message along its way.
One day the Earth will die,
Because of pollution
Gobbling up the Earth,
Like it was apple pie!

Georgia Hill (11)
Marchwood Junior School

War

War is knocking on your door
Calling your dads to come to more
Tell this war to stop knocking on your door
Then this world will live a lot more.

If this world lives a lot more
Then we would have time to sort
Our world of homeless people
And reduce, reuse, recycle things

This war is calling your dads
And some of our dads are dying
If we stop this war
It will be a law to stop war
If we do stop we will have peace
We would be friends with everyone
Including Greece, Afghanistan, Pakistan and Iraq
We would all be friends, just like me and Jack.

Cullan Mitchell (9)
Marchwood Junior School

Think Before You Act

Poachers being greedy
Animals becoming needy!

Animals are terrified, in fear
Don't be mean to deer.

The ice caps are melting
The polar caps are drowning.

The whales are being captured
While their bones are being fractured.

Have you ever thought
How many whales you are killing
When you put your lipstick on?

Charly-Jane Currie & Hettie Beale (11)
Marchwood Junior School

Go Green!

The planet's getting hotter and hotter and hotter,
Because of global warming and pollution,
So here's a way to change it -
  Go green!

Don't throw rubbish in the black sack,
Why don't you recycle it instead?
You can recycle paper, plastic, cardboard and carrier bags,
Don't be a global monster,
  Go green!

Cause all that rubbish goes to landfill sites,
And it stays there for ever and ever,
And there's more and more of it coming in,
And it needs more and more space, till the world will be
                                         trashed up so,

  Go green!

Ellie Bennett (8)
Marchwood Junior School

Being Homeless

People - sad as broken toys.
Cold weather - like a thousand knives.
Pavement - like a rocky mountain.
Rain - like the tears they cry.
Bus shelter - towering over the ignored tramp.
Money - calling for the homeless.

Man sees him,
Take my hand and step out
Of the darkness and into the light,
Walk on the streets with me.

Perry Whitmarsh & Danielle Meffen (11)
Marchwood Junior School

Animals And You

Animals are important to me,
But are they to you?
Help me do what's right for you!
The animals will be happy with you,
Help them now,
Come take my hand and I will help you.

Birds, dogs, cats and more are dying,
So help them all.
If you want to help come with me
And I will make you jump with glee!

Thanks for helping,
I hope you now feel happy.
So help them, save them, make them happy,
Come on everyone, come and join me!

Zoe Long (9)
Marchwood Junior School

Litter

Litter, litter, what horrible litter.
All those bins, searching for litter, starve without their food.
Someone, put the litter in the bin,
Please do.
Litter, litter, what horrible litter,
Cigarette butts fall on the ground,
Making dogs and cats sick.
Litter, litter, what horrible litter,
Make your way to the bin.

Solomon Carr (10)
Marchwood Junior School

Save The World

Look at the world, what can you see?
A homeless person.
Give them some money,
You will feel good.

Look at the world, what can you see?
Lots of rubbish,
Clean it up, it's nicer.

Look at the world, the world, what can you see?
Endangered animals, annoyed and scared,
Don't shoot them down or keep them in cages,
Just leave them alone.

Rory Clements (10)
Marchwood Junior School

Homeless

So tired, so lost,
All they want is a friend
Help them, help them
Save them again.

So sad, so cold,
So hungry, so old,
Why do people have to deal with this?
Save them, help them.

So long, so cold, no friend,
Like life's going to end,
Help them, save them,
Be a good friend.

Abigail Dodds (10)
Marchwood Junior School

Homeless Children

Look into the world,
What can you see?
Homeless children maybe.
They have no home,
They have no food.
Help them, help them!

Look into the world,
What can you see?
Homeless children maybe.
So ill, so lost, so tired, so hungry.
Help them, help them,
Love them, love them!

Look into the world,
What can you see?
Homeless children maybe.
They don't go to school,
They don't live in a house,
Send them something,
Then they won't be so ill.
Help them, help them!
Love them, love them!
Care for them, care for them!

Kimberley Collins (10)
Marchwood Junior School

Animals In Extinction

A nimals in agony
N asty hunters
 I n the wild animals killed
M eat eaters
A ll dying
L iving forever
S hooting animals.

Maisie White & Emma Horsefield (8)
Marchwood Junior School

Save Our Animal World

Animals, animals, animals,
What have they done to you?
Using cars, causing pollution,
Melting their only habitat,
Save them, save them.

Animals, animals, animals,
Wonderful creatures,
They may not be here,
If we don't see it clear,
Save them, save them.

Animals, animals, animals,
They have done nothing,
Why are we killing them?
Destroying their homes?
Save them, save them!

Matthew Edwards (10)
Marchwood Junior School

Animals

I wake up to the sound of birds cheeping,
I wake up to the sound of guns shooting.

I go to my wardrobe and get dressed,
I have to creep to not get shot.

I have a nice warm breakfast put under my nose,
I have cold meat covered in flies.

I go to school and make new friends,
I walk around the rubbish ends.

Some are lucky, some are not,
What could you do to help?

Charlotte Warner (10)
Marchwood Junior School

Poor, Poor Endangered Animals

E lephants are friendly so should be allowed to stay
N ever litter because it hurts animals
D ump your litter somewhere else not in the animals' ways
A nteaters only eat ants so why hurt them?
N asty people never think before they do
G iraffes are harmless so why hurt their feelings?
E ndangered animals do nothing wrong so why make
them sad?
R eal animals have got to live in trash too
E very day
D on't hurt animals just because they're in your way.

S nakes need compost so let them have it
P olar bears are nice so why ruin their icebergs?
E agles don't dump litter where we live so why should
we do it?
C aptured for life in extinction
I n places it's not fair for animals to live
E ach and every one of us need respect including the animals
S adly we might not have enough time but if we start now
we might be able to do something.

Katie Wood & Ria Twine (9)
Marchwood Junior School

Extinction!

E xtinct animals,
X -rayed animals can cause death,
T wo hundred animals die,
I cebergs are melting,
N ature is dying,
C reatures mean the world to us.
T wo animals dying, is two thousand animals dying,
I cebergs are killing lots of animals,
O pen your heart,
N o animals means more or less.

Amy Fielding & Danielle Anderson-Webb (9)
Marchwood Junior School

I Wake Up

I wake up to the sound of the trees
Swaying in the wind.

I wake up to the sound of horns
Beeping in the background.

My bed feels so warm.
My bed feels like a box of prickly straw.

I go to school and meet my best friends.
I have to look after my family.

I go and play outside with next door.
I can't go outside, I might get killed.

I have a warm fresh dinner.
I go and find some scraps.

Some children are lucky, some are not,
What could you do to help?

Hannah Curtis (9)
Marchwood Junior School

Five Polar Bears

Five polar bears playing tag,
One man came along and took one away for its fur.

Four polar bears having a sleep,
One man came along and shot one dead.

Three polar bears walking around,
One man came and he was gone.

Two polar bears playing ball,
One got trapped and then there was one.

One polar bear on his own,
One man came along, oh no!

Michael Guy (9)
Marchwood Junior School

Stop The Gas In The Air

10 risky planes hovered over
 9 days of loud sirens
 8 days of dreadful smoke
 7 days of wounded people
 6 days of teamwork
 5 days of smelly bombs
 4 days of starving hunger
 3 days of sad death
 2 days of serious battle
 1 day of sad lonely people
 0 - war is dreadful.

Dan Colmer (9)
Marchwood Junior School

Battle

10 days of bloodshed
 9 days of gas
 8 days of hunger
 7 days of bullets
 6 days of tears
 5 days of tanks
 4 days of death
 3 days of explosion
 2 days of the trench
 1 day of life
 0 - war is horrible.

Christy Towers (9)
Marchwood Junior School

War

I wake up to the shining of the sun.
I wake up to the sound of AKs blaring.
I go to a warm shower.
I go to the army and reload my weapon.
I go downstairs and watch TV.
I go to the meeting room and discuss our plan.
I go to work and get paid well.
I go to war and get paid little.
I go to a party and watch my friend have fun.
I'm in the middle of Afghanistan and watch my friend die.
I go home and go to bed.
I just carry on shooting.

Thomas Austin (10)
Marchwood Junior School

War

10 planes set off
 9 planes come back
 8 enemies set off gas bombs
 7 people stabbed
 6 guns shot
 5 first aiders run out
 4 TVs have news
 3 tanks blow up
 2 people get set on fire
 1 person left on the world.

Jamie Pidgley (9)
Marchwood Junior School

The World

If we keep polluting,
The ozone will be gone.

We'll be roasting,
And there'll be oceans down to a puddle.

Wasting water is a crime,
You could put animals on the line.

While we relax in our cool baths,
Think of all the other who don't have water
To waste like that, therefore,
Don't have as many great privileges.

Imagine waking up on a bench alone.
Imagine looking round and all the trees were gone.

If everyone was good and did what they should,
The world could be saved.

Leah Perkis (10)
Marchwood Junior School

War

10 days of bullets aimed at people.
 9 people wounded and dead.
 8 tanks launching rockets.
 7 medics in arms.
 6 planes dropping troops and supplies.
 5 hand grenades thrown through a cracked window.
 4 troops are dying from explosions.
 3 soldiers lay down in scratchy mud.
 2 helicopters fire at and crash.
 1 bomb blows up.

Thomas Robinson (9)
Marchwood Junior School

Save Animals

Please stop cutting down trees,
I'm telling you please.
Keep the Earth ever so clean,
So stop being mean.

Stop traffic from being bad,
You're driving the world mad.
Well done for the recycling,
Just keep on trying.

Don't do racism every day nor ever,
So that's that.
All the animals are so sad,
You're making vets so sad.

Ice breaking,
People taking,
We are losing land.
So help us.

Daniel Reed (10)
Marchwood Junior School

What People Do To Animals

10 giraffes dying from darts and being eaten
 9 nasty people killing cute snow tigers every day
 8 noisy bombs shocking all the animals in the jungle
 7 spotty leopards being heartbroken from not being fed
 6 homeless upset monkeys climbing trees
 5 scary cuts the orang-utans are dying from
 4 cuddly pandas extinct from climbing trees
 3 crazy gorillas jumping for their lives
 2 days of hungry dolphins swimming underwater
 1 sad poorly zebra trying to save its life.

Leila Wallingford & Charlotte Landy (9)
Marchwood Junior School

Stop Racism

Religious people getting laughed at
All the people with coloured skin getting laughed at
Sleeping people on benches getting laughed at
Ill people with diseases getting laughed at
Scared people getting laughed at
Muslims getting laughed at

Stop laughing
Start
Respecting.

Tristan Orchard (8)
Marchwood Junior School

Untitled

Don't throw your litter on the ground
Don't throw your litter on nature
Don't throw your litter in forests
Always put litter in the bin
Don't throw your litter in rabbit holes
Don't throw rubbish in bushes
Please save our world.

Zoe Carroll
Marchwood Junior School

Animals

A bandoned beautiful animals
N o more lives for the lovely animals
I love animals
M ammals like a whale
A nimals are gorgeous
L ives are lovely
S eals are pretty.

Charlotte White
Marchwood Junior School

Look At Us

Look at us, look at us, see what you've done,
Look at us, please be kind and see what has become.
Look at the gentle giant that swims in the sea,
Don't hurt them, don't hunt them and if you see one,
See what you can do to help them if you can.
Look at the creature that runs fast, it's a cheetah,
People kill them for their skin.
Look at the eagle on the cliff edge, isn't he beautiful?
But some people shoot them down, *poor thing,* you think.
Look, please look at them, they're desperate to live,
So please look at them, what have they done to us?

Gracie Rose Walker (9)
Marchwood Junior School

Please Recycle

Please, please don't throw your trash
You will hurt us animals
The fox, the monkey and especially the horse
So please, please be careful
Just throw your trash away
Because if you don't we die every single day.

Lisa Martin (9)
Marchwood Junior School

City Of Cars

In the world there is a city,
In the city there are some cars.
In the car there is some harmful gas,
The gas pollutes the Earth,
The Earth is saying,
Don't pollute me or we'll all die,
If we stop polluting then we'll save me!

William Trueman (8)
Marchwood Junior School

Stop The War

10 days of blood and smells
 9 days of death and sadness
 8 days of crying and help
 7 days of explosion and bombs
 6 days of noises and mist
 5 days of sorry and smoke
 4 days of dead and going home
 3 days of anger and sick
 2 days of mud and guts
 1 day to stop all the wars
No days to come back to life in the world.

Matthew Besant (9)
Marchwood Junior School

SOS

Help the world! Reuse, recycle, it helps *us.*
Save the world or it will hurt *us.*

 S ave the Earth before it's too late,
 O zone layer is going, the
 S un will fry and flood us.

Dean Kuyser (9)
Marchwood Junior School

Polluting The World

If the animals could speak, what would they say?
Stop polluting the world!

If the trees could speak, what would they say?
Stop polluting the world!

If the world could speak, what would it say?
Stop polluting me!

George Hibbs (9)
Marchwood Junior School

Dangerous Waters

D readful waters all over Africa,
I f you stop it they won't have diseases.
R emember there are people dying every day,
T hat if you helped them they wouldn't get ill,
Y ou wouldn't like it.

W aters are dangerous and full of nasty diseases,
A re you going to help?
T ogether it would make a difference.
E ager for clean, clear water,
R emember, help them!

Lucy Tilt (9)
Marchwood Junior School

What Would You Do?

What would you do if you were the last of your kind?
How would you feel if you were the world getting burnt?
What would you do if you were in a forest fire?
How would you feel if you had no home?
What would you do if you were in a war zone?
How would you feel if sewage was chucked in your home?

Ellie Penk (8)
Marchwood Junior School

War

Can you hear the gunfire killing all the people?
Can you hear the blood drops dripping on the ground?
Can you see the huge tanks blowing up everything?
Can you see homes getting knocked down?
Can you hear the cries trying to get fierce?
Can you hear the generals shouting out, 'No'?
The motto of this is you can help to stop this
By helping the less fortunate to a better life.

Jack Whetren (10)
Marchwood Junior School

Pollution

P ollution is making our world come to an end
O ur animals are becoming extinct because of you
L and is becoming dangerous for our animals
L and animals are being killed for their fur
U nderstand the people who say recycle
T ransform recycled materials into new plastic objects
I nch by inch the world is becoming polluted
O lder animals cannot get away from danger as fast
    as the little ones
N ature is in danger, we need your help.

Neisha Rendell (9)
Marchwood Junior School

Go Green!

In the world there is a forest,
In the forest there is an animal,
In the animal there is a cut,
In the cut there is sharp plastic,
In the plastic there are germs,
Save our world!
Put the plastic in a recycling bin,
Put the recycling in a factory,
Make something new,
    Recycle!

Abigail Deane (9)
Marchwood Junior School

Life

If animals could speak what would they say?
People all around, stop cutting down our habitats.

If the air could speak what would it say?
Please stop putting pollution in us.

If rivers could speak what would they say?
Stop putting rubbish in us, it's horrible and disgusting.

If land could speak what would it say?
Please stop putting buildings on us for money.

Think about life.

Jack White (9)
Marchwood Junior School

The War

There was a war
In that war there was a man
In that man there was a heart
In that heart was a feeling
That feeling was a strong feeling
That feeling was a sad feeling
That feeling got stronger and sadder
That feeling went down until he was heartbroken.
    Please help!

Thomas Walsh (8)
Marchwood Junior School

Different Places

I wake up to my comfy bed.
They wake up to bullets overhead.

I have a lovely warm bath.
They walk twelve miles for dirty water.

I go downstairs for breakfast.
They walk to a dangerous factory.

I walk to school for education.
They pass away during the day.

We could make this world beautiful again,
But only if we supply food and water.

Evan Meadows (9)
Marchwood Junior School

Animals

Just think of animals dying because of mankind
People having to cut down trees to grow crops
Meaning animals have to leave
Poaching to feed their families and sell skin
So much rubbish is being put in the seas
Global warming, melting icebergs
Just think if you were me, waking up, walking 10 miles
                                        to get water,
How unfair would that be?

Jack Sardeña (10)
Marchwood Junior School

Other Life

I wake up in the morning
to the golden sun shining down on me.

I wake up in the morning
to find dead animals around my tent,
I feel sorry for them.

I get dressed, go for a walk
and breathe in the fresh air that surrounds me.

I go to work wearing the same clothes,
I work in a carpet factory,
it is very dangerous.

Sasha Owsnett (10)
Marchwood Junior School

What We Have, What They Have

I wear clean clothes and have shoes to wear.
I wear my dusty rags and have bare feet.
I have books and toys to play with all day.
I work and clean all day long.
I go to bed with the sound of trees.
I go to bed with the sound of shouting and storms.
I take a warm bath every day of the week.
I walk five miles for the dirty muddy water to drink.
I go to school and learn how to read.

Lucy Finch (10)
Marchwood Junior School

The Poem About The Waterfall

In the rainforest
I can see a wonderful waterfall,
I can hear the water gushing down,
over the pointy, strong, steel rocks.

I can touch the icy cold, clear water
that trickles down my arm.
I can smell fresh water
falling down the waterfall.

I can see the mini beast
crawling towards the waterfall.
I can see the animals talking to each other.
I can see the water splashing over the rocks.

I can touch the stones
that are wet from the water.
I can touch the frogs
hopping from one place to another.

Daisy-May Palmer (9)
Medina Primary School

The Rainforest

In the rainforest
I can hear the water crashing down the hill,
I can hear animals running away,
I can hear birds singing.

In the rainforest
I can see flamingos bathing in water like fish,
I can see animals like mice scurrying away,
I can see snakes slithering slowly.

In the rainforest
I can smell sticky animal poo,
I can smell sweet blossom,
I can smell fresh grass swaying.

Elizabeth Davis (8)
Medina Primary School

In The Rainforest

In the rainforest
I can hear the water
gushing over the waterfall.
I can hear the trees
when the wind blows.

In the rainforest
I can see the trees swaying
and their branches touching each other
like they are holding hands.
I can see the great green leaves reaching.

In the rainforest
I can smell the brightly coloured flowers.
In the rainforest I can smell the animals coming closer.
I can smell the leaves on the trees.

In the rainforest
I can touch the long swaying grass.
I can touch the rotting seeds
that fall from the trees.

Tilly Melda Westrope (8)
Medina Primary School

All Alone In The Rainforest

In the rainforest
I can feel the soft breeze of the wind.
I can see the bushy tree being blown.
I can hear the birds tweeting at each other.
In the rainforest
I can hear the crocodile snapping his jaws.
I can smell the dirty frogs right next to me.
In the rainforest
I can hear twigs snapping.
I can smell the bark on the old tree.
I can feel the bumps on the old tree.

William Slade (8)
Medina Primary School

In the Rainforest

In the rainforest
I can hear the water rushing down the stream.

In the rainforest
I can see monkeys swing from trees
And frogs hopping everywhere.

In the rainforest
I can smell the trees, flowers
And old leaves which sound squelchy.

In the rainforest
I can touch slimy wet leaves
That are dipping with condensation.

In the rainforest
Everything goes crazy
While you're tucked up in bed.

Rebecca Heath (8)
Medina Primary School

Rainforest

In the rainforest
I can feel the smooth plants swaying in the wind,
I can feel the small leaves on the tall trees as they fall on me.

In the rainforest
I can see the water rushing down the waterfall,
I can see dirty green frogs jumping from rock to rock.

In the rainforest
I can hear the footsteps from the enormous animals
As the monkeys swing from tree to tree.

In the rainforest
I can smell fresh grass growing on the hillside,
I can smell the animals' skin.

Holly Louise Legge (9)
Medina Primary School

Earth Has Many Feelings

Earth has many feelings, some sad and some full of joy,
Earth has many tastes, sweet, sour and plain,
Earth also has senses, sight, touch, hearing and smell.

Earth will be sad if you cut down trees,
Earth will be happy if you protect bees,
Earth finds it bitter if you drop litter,
But it is not the same as fallen fresh leaves.

Earth is just like you and me,
If you cut your finger,
That's what Earth feels like when you cut down a tree,
So if you leave the plants alone and respect the Earth,
The Earth will do the same for us,
You wait and see!

Charlotte Phillips (9)
Niton Primary School

War, Rainforests And Extinction

War, war, disgusting wars, let alone litter,
Rainforests and extinction.
All these bad things cannot go on for much longer,
If it does will no animals be left?
The world would belong to just one country!
Without any signs of life just rubbish around twenty metres high.
Recycling may help, agreeing may help
Not chucking litter everywhere may help
And replanting may help.

Ross Whyte (9)
Niton Primary School

An Endangered Poem

Though polar bears are endangered,
With snowy white fur and huge broad feet,
Mankind is still hunting these furry friends of ours.
Next comes the bald eagle who is a magnificent sight
But why do we hunt them just for our delight?
This is the lovely tapir, humans burn the rainforests with fire,
But what really is a tapir's heart's desire?

Kimberley Trasler (9)
Niton Primary School

Save The World

The trees are being cut down,
This idea makes me frown.

Pollution is ruining the brilliant sky,
This thought makes me cry.

War is rubbish, war is bad,
The idea of it makes me sad.

Throwing away is such a waste,
This idea isn't to my taste.

Help us if you've something to say,
So in the future we can shout *hooray!*

William Taylor (9)
St Mary's CE Junior School, Basingstoke

I'm A Scary Woodcutter

I'm a scary woodcutter, I'm as mean as can be.
I'm a scary woodcutter, I hate every tree.
I'm a scary woodcutter, animals go flee.
Trees get cut down, animals make a frown.
Everyone can tell our world is soon to be a second hell.

Charlie Lucas-Smith (9)
St Mary's CE Junior School, Basingstoke

Think World

T hought comes into your head,
H ateful things all around you,
I magine a place with nice things,
N o one caring for our world,
K illing animals and nature.

W e can help save the environment,
O ur cars making fumes,
R ecycling must keep up the pace,
L ittering must stop,
D oom to our world must die.

Merryn Heels (9)
St Mary's CE Junior School, Basingstoke

A Better World

Litter luncher
Bone cruncher
Waste won'ter
What am I?

Tree cruncher
Creature killer
Animal doomer
What am I?

Capryce Dunning (9)
St Mary's CE Junior School, Basingstoke

London Trees Are Falling Down

T hud, thud trees are falling
R ip, tear, people don't really care
E arth is dying, trees are falling
E co-kids are coming, help save trees before they crush you
S ave our environment before London trees start falling down.

Sam Western (8)
St Mary's CE Junior School, Basingstoke

World Destroyer

Oxygen destroyer
Rubbish maker
Animal home cruncher
Environment destroyer
Tree masher
Pollution machine
What am I?
I'm a logging machine.

Flower grower
Tree grower
Pollution stopper
Animal carer
World maker
What am I?
I'm the future.

Harriet Fern (9)
St Mary's CE Junior School, Basingstoke

Save Our World

S aving our world will be much better for nature.
A nyone can do it, just be a creator.
V arious people do it a lot.
E veryone should do it, just put it in a pot.

O ur world will die right away.
U nderground it is night-time all day.
R ecycle for the future.

W orld around us has pollution.
O ver and under the gas goes.
R abbits are dying, cars all around those.
L ots of pollution everywhere.
D ying and dying with a big scare!

Paul Surplice (9)
St Mary's CE Junior School, Basingstoke

Ebony And Ivory Stay United!

'Hi, I'm black.'
'Hi, I'm white.
Let's go out and play tonight.'
'What a nice suggestion, think that you might . . .'

That night Ebony got shot,
By the friend he thought he'd got.
Do you think Ivory's decision was right?
Just because he was black and not white.

But guns aren't the only thing invading our streets,
Its knives and their power that help them defeat.
Why is this happening? No one knows.
But it's one bad thing on Earth that has to go.

What about an age limit of which they can buy knives?
That would help to cut down half of the crime.
Guns are illegal to carry around at any time.
If you get caught with one without a licence
Prepare to be alone and in silence.

Rhianna Perkins (11)
St Mary's CE Junior School, Basingstoke

Do More To Recycle

R ecycling makes the world go round.
E nd all the litterbugs around us.
C ycle to the recycling bins but do not use a car.
Y o, we have to end this now.
C ycle everywhere and not a drop of petrol to spare.
L ine it out, that's what recycling is all about.
I will do something because littering is the worst.
N ice to recycle it all the time.
G as puddles everywhere.

PS . . . recycle today!

Georgia King (9)
St Mary's CE Junior School, Basingstoke

The Rainforest

R unning down the trees
A heap of moaning woodblocks
I t's thought to make guys pleased
N ot me I'm suffocating
F alling plants is anti-breathing
O r a dead animal
R idding them and you'll see
E ven air's dying for cash
S o you get to heave
T he dead animal you killed for dinner.

R eally it's too much
A tree-less planet's view
I t's easy to stop as such
N ot as hard as you thought
F ree the trees in the crutch
O r join the tree huggers
R ebuild it (you don't need to be Dutch)
E asy to stop these sounds
S hredding round the hutch
T he time is *now!*

Alexander Drewry (11)
St Mary's CE Junior School, Basingstoke

Pollution

P eople of the world should change.
O nly the cars can return to batteries.
L onely greens slowly turn brown.
L ost air fades away.
U p in the air it turns black.
T owns and cities try to help.
I do as much as I can.
O nly everyone can stop this pollution.
N o one should stop trying.

Abigail Fern (10)
St Mary's CE Junior School, Basingstoke

Save The Planet

S ave our planet.
A rrive in a brand new planet.
V arious trees are being cut down,
E at up pollution.

T his pollution is bad.
H ey mate it makes me sad.
E arth can be changed by you!

P ut all your litter in the bin!
L ook it kills animals, that's a sin.
A lways recycle.
N ot putting me in a rubbish pile.
E ven you can make a guess
T he world is a great big mess.

Aidan Day (9)
St Mary's CE Junior School, Basingstoke

A Better World

People waiting for a bus,
Not using a car,
Help our planet!

People putting in recycling bin,
Help our planet!

People planting new seeds,
Help our planet!

People using litter bins,
Help our planet!

All work and try together,
Help our planet!

Britney Boyd (8)
St Mary's CE Junior School, Basingstoke

Save Our World

S ave the planet by recycling
A sk us how we can change the world
V iolence stops
E arth can be nice.

O ur world can be changed
U could save everyone
R ecycling rules.

W hen you work on paper recycle it
O ur rubbish will be gone soon
R ecycling could save our lives
L earn not to waste useful things
D o help us recycle.

Michael Ash (9)
St Mary's CE Junior School, Basingstoke

Hedgehog Habitat

I'm a hedgehog,
My mate got ran over yesterday.
So why can't everyone
Just walk and say,
Stop pollution, stop littering.
I fell in oil, trust me it hurts,
Right outside me house,
Oh and so did Bert.

My message today is all I've got to say,
Walk don't drive
Cos it's not nice!

Jordan Lodomez (9)
St Mary's CE Junior School, Basingstoke

Save Your Future

S ave our animals from dying,
A nimals are killed, I start crying.
V ery rare animals are becoming extinct,
E veryone can help; if only they just think!

A ll animals will eventually become rare,
N ot if we can help; they won't become scarce.
I t's not just animals, it's trees as well,
M any will die; *dong* goes the church bell.
A nimals are being cruelly suffocated,
L itter is the culprit, animals are being baited.
S o do something to save animals and trees.

It's your future so please
Help save the Earth!

Helen Frawley (11)
St Mary's CE Junior School, Basingstoke

Save Animals

S ave Earth
A lways recycle
V ocals making speeches
E arth needs to see them

A nimals are dying
N o littering
'I need help,' the animals cry
M ake the world a good place
A pes need the most help
L et us live
S ave animals.

Jamie MacQuillin (8)
St Mary's CE Junior School, Basingstoke

Future World!

Blood-shedder
Tear-dropper
Bone-breaker
Land-crusher
Earth-destroyer
Life-killer . . .
What am I?
I am war!

Flower-crusher
Tree-chopper
Animal-killer
Bone-breaker
Feather-plucker . . .
What am I?
I am an animal killer!

Litter-searcher
School-walker
Animal-adopter
People-carer
Blood-stopper
Life-saver . . .
What am I?

The future world!

Tayla Porter (10)
St Mary's CE Junior School, Basingstoke

Care For Animals

We need to help animals get their lives back,
They're very upset and extremely hurt,
Please stop killing animals, they need some help.
Let rhinos have some food,
They really need some friends and some parents,
So please help the parents.

Jasmine Symonds (8)
St Mary's CE Junior School, Basingstoke

Littering

L itterbugs are messy
I 'm amazed that people do it
T he pollution is spreading
T he animals are getting hurt
E veryone stop littering
R eading newspapers then throwing them on the ground
I t's bad to litter
N ever be a litterbug
G o away litterbugs, go away!

Amy Hermitage (9)
St Mary's CE Junior School, Basingstoke

Racing To Recycle

R ecycling is caring for the environment,
E specially bottles and cans,
C reatively bottles can be made into beads.
Y our cardboard can also be recycled.
C an you see a green bin?
L ots of trucks with dustbin men.
I am going to recycle!
N ever throw stuff away that can be recycled.
G oing to race to recycle!

Katie Guo (8)
St Mary's CE Junior School, Basingstoke

Stop Racism!

'R eligion is the problem,' they say
A ge might be a problem
C hrist is some people's belief
I f they don't like you
S ome people believe in different things
M en are black and white.

Jacob Bell (8)
St Mary's CE Junior School, Basingstoke

Pollution

Pollution, pollution, o' stop pollution . . .

Car using
Fuel wasting
Fire burning
Health losing
Bone cruncher
Bomb disaster
Plane user
Tree cutter
Grenade explosion.

Try this instead . . .

Pool diving
Party sharing
Walking or running
Jogging
Ball shooting
Basketball shot
Hockey goaling
More trees
I think that's better!

Aaron Randall (9)
St Mary's CE Junior School, Basingstoke

The Polluted World

Animals dying out
Engines giving carbon dioxide
Oil rigs being damaged
Less trees
Less oxygen
Using more electricity
Explosives polluting the world
More CO_2 being produced.

Harrison Crass (9)
St Mary's CE Junior School, Basingstoke

The World's Climate!

Climate change is affecting our world,
CO_2 is a barrier we must break through,
My disappointment will soon be unfurled,
God is boiling because of His Earth changing crew!

Animals are suffering from our ungreen ways,
Ice is melting because of us,
The sun is struggling to control its exploding rays,
Help and . . . *stop climate change!*

Jordan Thorne (9)
St Mary's CE Junior School, Basingstoke

Who Am I?

I live in a dark street, who am I?
I have no money, who am I?
I search the bins, who am I?
I have dirty, ripped clothes, who am I?
I have no home, who am I?
I am wet and cold, who am I?
My legs are dirty, who am I?
I am a homeless child.

Robert Sheldrake (9)
St Mary's CE Junior School, Basingstoke

Poor People

P oor, they are on the street
O w a smelly place they live
V ery poor they are and no money in sight
E njoying of life soon to come
R usty and dusty are the streets
T o help we must because it is right
Y ou can help.

Holly Vary (9)
St Mary's CE Junior School, Basingstoke

What Am I? Kennings

Bone cruncher
Hole digger
Ball chewer
Man licker
Ragger puller
Pillow ripper
Hand chewer
What am I?

Food muncher
Ball hogger
Fast runner
Blood licker
Big dribbler
Food chewer
Ball catcher
Cat chase
What am I?

Lucy Bradley (9)
St Mary's CE Junior School, Basingstoke

Rainforest

R espect the trees
A nimals' homes
I mperial trees
N ever kill trees
F orever the trees will stand
O nly old trees should be chopped down
R ainforests should be saved
E xtinction of rainforests
S ave trees' lives
T ry to stop tree cutters.

Luke Briggs (9)
St Mary's CE Junior School, Basingstoke

The World Used To Be A Dream

The world used to be a dream,
Trees, animals and streams.
But now in this modern age
The world has really changed.
It makes me sick to see the world in this state
With all these cars polluting the place,
What a disgrace.

But there is a solution
And it isn't that hard,
All you have to do
Is grow your own food,
Not a lot just a little
Will do its bit;
Like a hero a carrot could be,
If you grow it yourself you'll get some glee
As a plane won't have to go to the shops
And dump some pollution,
It must stop!

Ashley Payne (11)
St Mary's CE Junior School, Basingstoke

Rainforest Lives

R espect animals and trees
A nimals' homes
I mperiled animals will live if we care
N eed help for lives and food
F orever the trees will stand
O nly chop dead trees
R abid animals, care for them
E xtinction
S ave lives
T omorrow what will it be like?

Matthew Comer (9)
St Mary's CE Junior School, Basingstoke

Stop It!

I've got one thing to say
To help the world today!
Go out for a walk!
Don't hang around and talk!
Get down to business!

Don't waste your litter
It makes the world look bitter!
Turn off your light,
It's still quite bright!
Get down to business!

Trees are crying for fresh air like a wailing child!
It makes the world more wild!
Boohoo
To you!
You're littering the Earth
When you gave birth!
Get down to business!

Hannah Duncanson (10)
St Mary's CE Junior School, Basingstoke

Detonating Wars

Soldiers are dying, fighting for life
I see people getting shot, stabbed by knife
The war has started, there's bad blood between
The skull and crossbones is not far to be seen
We all want peace, just let go and release
Freedom is in the air
Now we all want to care
It's better to care
Let's keep it there.

Lenny Rice (9)
St Mary's CE Junior School, Basingstoke

World Sources!

P ollution no more
E scape from war
A ll habitats are destroyed
C hange for the world
E veryone will die one day.

T urn over a new leaf
O ther countries are very sick.

T he world needs our care
H appiness is needed to others
E veryone accept the consequences.

W hat does the world mean to you?
O ur home is the world
R ecycling is helpful
L ife is ours
D iseases leave us or children and adults will be deceased.

Georgia Freeman (9)
St Mary's CE Junior School, Basingstoke

Use Less Cars

U se your legs.
S ome people and animals die because of pollution.
E ven when we try to stop pollution it keeps coming back.

L ess cars, less pollution.
E vil pollution.
S top pollution.
S top killing the atmosphere.

C ars kill the atmosphere
A nd cars kill plants and animals.
R ip pollution out.
S ometimes it kills people.

Tom Turner (9)
St Mary's CE Junior School, Basingstoke

A Glorious World?

Earth is dying
Because of poverty,
Rejected, lost and lonely.
Children are suffering
With nowhere to go,
No one to talk to
And all alone . . .

Starving and thirsty,
Dying and fading
From this dreaded world,
With a final curse . . .
Of death.

Eating rubbish,
Nothing else,
Will kill these children,
With their final words
Of hope, faith and justice . . .

Needing help,
Struggling for life
And for a perfect normal life,
What would you do?

Christy Chui (11)
St Mary's CE Junior School, Basingstoke

Crazy War!

Spitfire launching
Rifle leaping
Machine gun roaring
Grenade banging
Missiles following
With your head
Helicopter hell
Happiness fell
When is it going to end?

Jack Randall (9)
St Mary's CE Junior School, Basingstoke

Third World Diseases

Coughs and sneezes
Spread diseases,
People need protection
By a life-saving injection.

Staying still
In bed ill,
Life and death
One last breath.

Families shatter,
Nothing matters,
The Third World crave
For medical aid.

They need food and drink
To get off the brink,
To help stop
The awful shock.

The shipment sold
To young and old.
It's as quick as a race
At a cheetah's pace.

Edward Quick (11)
St Mary's CE Junior School, Basingstoke

Pollution

P ollution is bad
O ld people are worried
L ove always recycles
L ovely little monkeys in the rainforest
U se buses more
T ry and not use cars
I f you love smoking stop
O h turn the light off
N ow stop smoking.

Daisy Potter (8)
St Mary's CE Junior School, Basingstoke

Contaminating Beauty

Loathing, despair
We terrorise our humble Earth.
Call a halt to driving destructive automobiles,
We have legs.

Toxic whiffs cause death,
Odours can kill.
Descend your bags and bottles to the earthly floor,
Making our planet hideous.

Polluting and littering is terribly wrong,
Refrain from this (and everything else).
We live here, we eat here, we want to stay here,
Help us, the eco-kids, make the right decision.

Maddie Merwin (11)
St Mary's CE Junior School, Basingstoke

Save The Animals

Stop killing all the animals
And feel sorry for the mammals.
Help them now
And give them a bow.
Don't let them down,
Don't give them a frown.

Stop breaking their habitats,
You just can't do that.
Keep up the trees,
Oh please, please, please.
Let the animals have a breeze
But don't let them freeze.

Tash Porter (9)
St Mary's CE Junior School, Basingstoke

Rainforest Protester's Problems

Kingdom-slasher,
Tree-pusher,
Flat-splatter,
Oil-spacer,
Acre-smasher,
Nature-killer.
I am a JCB.

Love-maker,
Peace-bringer,
Problem-stopper,
Hard-trier,
Desperate-holder,
Animal-supporter.
I am a protester.

Charlie Taylor (11)
St Mary's CE Junior School, Basingstoke

Earth's Agony

Poverty leads to homelessness,
Another world issue,
Littering leaves, quite a mess,
As much as a simple tissue.

Clothes are turned to rags,
People look bitter,
All their clothes in bags,
Still people just litter.

Scars spread on a face,
Ripped and torn away,
Such a wonderful place
Is ruined in a day.

James Ash (11)
St Mary's CE Junior School, Basingstoke

Litter

L ess dropping
I n the bins
T ry not to drop
T ell someone
E xtinction of animals
R emember

No litter!

Georgia Beard (8)
St Mary's CE Junior School, Basingstoke

Helping

H elp the world
E veryone, stop littering
L ittering is bad
P eople keep polluting
I think extinction is on the way
N othing can stop it
G round falling from the sky.

Daniel Cochrane (8)
St Mary's CE Junior School, Basingstoke

Helpless

People are homeless
In the street they are breathless
But we are careless.

People are dying
But we rich must be lying
We are still crying.

We have things to give
But we also want to live
They can have my sieve.

Charles Robertson (11)
St Mary's CE Junior School, Basingstoke

Pollution

P ark your car
O nly use your car if you have to
L ose the car
L ight off when you are not in a room
U nder your nose pollution is spreading
T rees are like humans, if you kill a tree it is like killing a human
I n some parts of the sea it is like being in a tank of oil
O il kills, don't dump it!
N ever litter or dump rubbish.

Daniel Weir (11)
St Mary's CE Junior School, Basingstoke

Poisonous Pollution

Foul littering is careless,
Disgusting and laziness,
Litter everywhere to be seen,
Wherever I have been.

Pollution is poisonous,
Illegal and fearless,
Toxic gas is not far away,
Which is happening every day.

Jonathan Hyam (11)
St Mary's CE Junior School, Basingstoke

Impact On Animals

As trees cry out in pain,
As animals' homes are hit like a cane,
As the deadly litter touches the ground, not the bin,
Begins a din.
So, people of the world think before you do,
And start animals' life anew.

Fraser McGregor (10)
St Mary's CE Junior School, Basingstoke

Save The Day!

The Earth is watching you today
Please help, climate change, it's on the way
It is no fault of us
It's you, riding in a car or bus.

Walk that mile or two
Leave your car in the garage
Fine, run to school but don't run ravage.

Okay, thanks for your help
That's all you can do
You've done what we asked
How good are you!

Ryan Cochrane
St Mary's CE Junior School, Basingstoke

War

War is murder,
War is death,
Don't copy Bond
On the TV set.

Guns and knives
Never work,
But if you use them
They can hurt.

Gangs are bad,
Gangs are violent,
If you carry a weapon with no licence
Prepare for a long and lonely silence.

Matthew Parry (9)
St Mary's CE Junior School, Basingstoke

My Poem

People keep cutting down loads of trees for paper,
Rainforests being chopped down too.

Habitats being destroyed,
It makes people upset and animals very annoyed.

In waste sites it smells so bad,
It makes people sad.

Diseases are being caught from rats,
So that makes people and animals very ill.
Some can die from it.

People are destroying habitats,
So this means that there are becoming
Less and less animals in the world.

The world is running
Out of room for everything.

Hannah Best (10)
St Mary's CE Junior School, Basingstoke

Improve

Nuclear bombs
People dying
Environment crushed
We should improve
Recycle
No wars
No diseases
No trees cut
Friends, peace
It should be that.

Reece Simper (10)
St Mary's CE Junior School, Basingstoke

Save The Animals And Trees

All around the world,
Creatures are going extinct,
Habitats are seized.

It's like an orange,
All the bad gets peeled off,
If you help do it.

Homes are dragged away,
After fainting rapidly,
Habitats are dying.

When the trees go *bang,*
It is very upsetting,
You should recycle.

Waste is on the floor,
Litter is strangling creatures,
Even far away.

You can save Earth,
By not spreading litter,
And not hurting trees.

Please help save Earth,
The animals and rare trees,
It helps you and me.

Naomi Hughes-White (11)
St Mary's CE Junior School, Basingstoke

Disease

D isgraceful death-ray
I t's not funny
S uccessful lives have been saved
E veryone is trying to help
A ll people do is give medicine to them and it works
S ome people say give them the kiss of life and it works
E nding to take them to hospital.

Alice Senior (11)
St Mary's CE Junior School, Basingstoke

Racism

Black or white
You have the right,
Speak out
About . . .
Racism.

Communities mixed,
Racism ditched,
Speak out
About . . .
Racism.

Martin Luther King
Never gave in
All because he
Disagreed with . . .
Racism.

Racism the disease
Can be eased
If everyone
Gets along
No matter their
Race, religion, age,
Together
We can stop . . .
Racism.

James Alford (11)
St Mary's CE Junior School, Basingstoke

2008

E nough people and dying
A nd women are crying
R escue people are on the go
T he kids are crying
H ospitals are full and patients are dying.

Jordan Ward (10)
St Mary's CE Junior School, Basingstoke

The Solution For Pollution

Pollution, pollution,
Is so very bad,
But there is a solution,
So it isn't so sad.

Gases and fumes,
Spreading in the air,
Just like balloons,
So we have to care.

So walk to school,
Have some fun,
Stop polluting
And so,
My poem is done.

Rhys John Poole (10)
St Mary's CE Junior School, Basingstoke

Save Our Planet

This is what is happening now . . .
Power and gas breaking the ice and ozone,
Boilers breaking,
Gas escaping!
Mining for gold in Earth's old core,

Please save the ozone
Or the sun will start piercing
Without meaning to . . .
Save our planet!

Dominic Rodriguez (10)
St Mary's CE Junior School, Basingstoke

2008 Pollution, 2012 Olympics

2008 Pollution

Plane pollution
Nuclear pollution
Car pollution
Fuel pollution
It all adds up to global warming.

2012 Olympics

2012 Olympics
It's going to be great
Wembley Stadium
Tube station
Beaming with thousands of people.

Joseph Lane (10)
St Mary's CE Junior School, Basingstoke

My Recycling Poem

R ecycling
E asy
C hange the way we think
Y ou can recycle everywhere
C hallenge companies to recycle
L et them know we recycle but the companies don't help
I think we should recycle
N ever chuck away stuff you can recycle
G row and learn to recycle a brand new and better world *today.*

Amy Lillis (9)
St Mary's CE Junior School, Basingstoke

Stopping War

S top the war or else
T ons of people will die
O n the day they started
P ollution will happen when we make weapons
P ollution is bad
I nnocents will get murdered because of the war
N othing will survive if we don't make peace
G angs will learn from

W ind is cold and dusty
A ir pollution with gas
R unning, people going around so if I were you
    I'd better be doing something.

Aldouz Parnada (10)
St Mary's CE Junior School, Basingstoke

Can We Stop Now?

Things that shouldn't happen
Are taking place right now
And those who are responsible
Are causing a great big row.

Don't you think we should stop
Causing lots of trouble
Because inconsiderate people
Are going to burst my bubble?

Climate change is occurring
Meaning habitats are being destroyed
And people who aren't doing anything
Are making me annoyed.

Bethany Layland (10)
St Mary's CE Junior School, Basingstoke

Save Our World

Our world is being destroyed
Doesn't that make you annoyed?
They cut down trees and more disease
We've got to do something about it!

The world's pollution is increasing
But we don't realise what we're releasing
Into the air a gas I can't bear
It's taking the home of wildlife.

If global warming upsets you
And you're not sure what to do
Walk more or recycle
Cos we need your help!

Georgia Beeston (11)
St Mary's CE Junior School, Basingstoke

Can't We Do Anything?

People all over the world
Are experiencing global warming.
Although they try to make it stop
Others just sit there waiting.

Climate change is ruining our world
While we are eating our dinner.
Little do we know
That our world is growing thinner.

Can't we stop pollution?
Just quit using cars?
Many people don't know
That doing so, we'll go far.

Aditya Shrestha (11)
St Mary's CE Junior School, Basingstoke

Pollution Is Bad

P ollution is bad,
O h so sad,
L ets people down,
L ike a boring play,
U nder the atmosphere,
T he pollution never stops,
I n the air,
O ver the skies . . . the pollution continues,
N ever pollute.

Dickson Chui (10)
St Mary's CE Junior School, Basingstoke

Living Things!

Is it good to be extinct?
No I don't think it is.
Do you want to be hunted down?
No.
How do you think animals feel?
Lonely, upset, with fear in their soul.
What can they do?
Nothing but if we act now we can save
Living things!

Jemma Godleman (10)
St Mary's CE Junior School, Basingstoke

Destruction Of The Earth

Sadness sweeps his hand
Over vast black land
That place is where I stand
Trees and animals have died or fled
Now that our once beautiful land is dead.

Jody Patton (11)
St Mary's CE Junior School, Basingstoke

How Can We Help The World

Rubbish in the streets,
Scattered everywhere.
One person picks up the rubbish,
He puts it in the bin.
Now it's tidy.
Cars pollute the air.
People shout out, 'We don't care.'
People get walking it helps the world.
Now it's over,
Remember help the world.

James Smith-Cumming (11)
St Mary's CE Junior School, Basingstoke

Poverty

P oor people
O f the world
V ans and cars going by looking at the people on the streets
E veryone is homeless shouting for help
R unning, jumping on people's cars
T hinking they will let them stay
Y elling help, help.

Charlie-Louise Batchelor (11)
St Mary's CE Junior School, Basingstoke

Water Wasters

W ater is a precious thing so be careful what you do.
A fter brushing your teeth turn off the tap.
T aking the fishes home is a horrible crime.
E ver thought of stopping CO_2?
R estoring their territory is always a good thing.

Hannah Toogood (11)
St Mary's CE Junior School, Basingstoke

War And Peace

W ary of what will happen next,
A ngrily wanting to stop,
R unning to the fort.

A nd knowing what he has to do next.
N ot wanting to fight,
D oing what he has to do.

P erhaps he may die.
E nergy rushing through him,
A nxious he might lose a friend,
C ourage escapes from him,
E erie silence. He's shot.

Will you help?

Ashleigh Rheann Jones (11)
St Mary's CE Junior School, Basingstoke

Changes

From land to sea,
Mountain to marsh,
Coast to coast,
Camp to hearth,
We carry a burden,
A blanket of fear,
The climate changes
Year on year,
But we can change
The world to be,
By making changes
We'll be free.

Andrew Gurr (11)
St Mary's CE Junior School, Basingstoke

Creatures Facing Death

Swimming through the ruined ocean
There's pollution, nets and litter.
We whales are in need of help
We're creatures facing death.

Striding through the threatened forest
Looking out for big cat traps.
Tigers hiding is no good
We're creatures facing death.

Running for my life again,
The third time in this week.
We foxes run from hunting dogs,
We're creatures facing death.

Sinead Grover (11)
St Mary's CE Junior School, Basingstoke

Cruelty To The Planet

Happy hunters hunt helpless hippos
People pollute poor panthers
Terrified trees taken down for paper
Receding rainforest, animals and plants rampage in rage
Litter lurks around a lemur's life choking it to death.

So if you read this book
By the Big Green Poetry Machine
You can have a look
Get some ideas
And help to save the planet!

Thomas Ash (11)
St Mary's CE Junior School, Basingstoke

The Polar Bear

Once strong and mighty polar bear,
Yet now so sad and in despair.
The temperature is rising fast,
The future is different from the past.
No ice caps shall survive,
Polar bears will drown in chaos.
Polar bears will be a loss.
This is such a waste,
Make haste.
Save our planet,
Please don't forget,
The animals need you,
Remember what I'm implying,
The world is slowly dying.

Lauren Nicholls (11)
St Swithun's Primary School, Portsmouth

Earth

Earth was a wonderful place
With birds singing
And fishes that were swimming.

Now Earth is a terrible place,
Everyone is being so careless
With food on the floor
And driving with pace.

Earth is still a beautiful place
But the nasty littering
Is affecting our place
So act now.

Corey Almond (9)
St Swithun's Primary School, Portsmouth

The Wolves

The wolves roam out
Ready to hunt.
The deer start grazing
Oblivious to the wolves.

The wolves pick out their prey,
Old and weak.
The deer look up,
But thinks it's nothing.

The wolves start prowling,
Slow and steady.
The deer still grazing,
But getting more alert.

The wolves close in,
Ready to pounce.
The deer look up,
More alert and watchful.

Then the wolves strike
Like a meteor falling to Earth.
The deer start running,
The chase is on.

The wolves are running,
The herd scatters.
The deer panic
And expose the targeted.

The wolves lock on
Like a demon homing missile.
The targeted deer will soon tire
As he runs for his life.

The wolf attacks
And strikes and hits.
The deer is wounded,
Fatally.

This will never happen again
If we do not let the wolves run free
Like they were to be.

Christopher Shore (9)
St Swithun's Primary School, Portsmouth

Recycle

R emember it is cool to recycle,
E ven if it's a bicycle.
C lever people do,
Y ou should do it to.
C lap and cheer,
L ose it or not, you will reuse it.
E ventually everyone will . . .

recycle!

Katie Dalgleish (11)
St Swithun's Primary School, Portsmouth

Pollution

Last afternoon I heard horns of cars making noises like cows.
I saw a huge line of cars going past very fast.
I knew they were a source of pollution, it stops evolution,
The car fumes flew higher and higher whilst getting thinner.
I knew where it would go but I couldn't make it low,
So that I could blow it into fresh air.
It rose up in the clouds until it was blocked and locked,
It thought and ate at the ozone layer, please make a stop to this.

Jistel Djeumo (11)
St Swithun's Primary School, Portsmouth

The Environment

There was once a beautiful world where animals were safe
And enjoyed their environment.

But that was the past and now many are endangered.
There are animals being killed right at this moment,
The minute you read this poem.

Have you ever thought about life?
I know it's cruel but this is the way we made it,
So do something,
Something to save the environment before it's too late!

Joseph Hargreaves (10)
St Swithun's Primary School, Portsmouth

Be A Superhero And Save The World

If it's a sunny day walk to school
You really know it's cool.

And if you recycle you won't really lose it
Because you can reuse it.

The world is spinning around every second
And getting dizzy and annoyed every day.

Please look after the world.
Be a superhero!

Annabel House (10)
St Swithun's Primary School, Portsmouth

Where Have They Gone?

Wolves used to roam the land
Searching far and wide,
But where have they gone?
Does anyone know? Did they get a ride?

Birds fly up high in the sky
Wondering when the day is nigh.
Must hide no time to spare,
Look out for that hunter there!

Jacob Hillman-Illingworth (10)
St Swithun's Primary School, Portsmouth

The Oak Tree

This oak tree is very special
And very ginormous.
It has ruffling leaves,
Ruffling branches all over
And smooth leaves.
The oak tree, the oak tree
Never runs away,
Always here, never runs away.

Niamh Colby (7)
St Swithun Wells Catholic Primary School

My Little, Funny Tree

I'm short and thin, lovely and rough,
I love the wind blowing onto my leaves,
Blowing all around me.
I don't really talk that much at all,
I really like to move around
But sadly I'm stuck to the ground.

Patrick Brewer (7)
St Swithun Wells Catholic Primary School

Our Earth

Our Earth needs to be loved,
So let's make it a better place,
Our Earth wants to be cared for,
Stop the violence,
Stop the wars,
Stop the killing,
Stop the madness,
Let's make peace on our Earth!

Our Earth needs to be loved,
So let's make it a better place,
Our Earth wants to be cared for,
Stop the people being homeless,
Stop the diseases,
Stop the poverty,
Stop the sadness,
Let's make love on our Earth!

Our Earth needs to be loved,
So let's make it a better place,
Our Earth wants to be cared for,
Stop the climate change,
Stop the pollution,
Stop the littering,
Stop the pain,
Let's make laughter on our Earth!

Our Earth needs to be loved,
So let's make it a better place,
Our Earth wants to be cared for,
Keep recycling,
Shield the rainforests,
Credit joy,
Praise happiness,
Let's make the Earth the best!

Matthew Moules (10) & James Davis (11)
St Swithun Wells Catholic Primary School

War

Why this fighting, why the war?
It's nothing that we asked for.
People crying, people in pain,
Stop this cruel and stupid game.

Destruction, destroying, lives have been taken,
Maybe this war is silly and mistaken,
Maybe not, maybe it's a dream,
Nightmare or not, we're still killing machines.

We've ripped lives apart with idiotic moves,
Standing for our rights, trying to prove
That we can get along if we really do try,
But sometimes we just give up and cry.

World War I, World War II,
How many wars will we get through?
Will we make it?
Will our hearts mend?
Or will the world come to an end . . .?

Melissa Dorrington (11)
St Swithun Wells Catholic Primary School

Young Writers Information

We hope you have enjoyed reading this book - and that you will continue to enjoy it in the coming years.

If you like reading and writing poetry drop us a line, or give us a call, and we'll send you a free information pack.

Alternatively if you would like to order further copies of this book or any of our other titles, then please give us a call or log onto our website at www.youngwriters.co.uk

Young Writers Information
Remus House
Coltsfoot Drive
Peterborough
PE2 9JX

(01733) 890066